STUDIES IN HISTORY, ECONOMICS AND
PUBLIC LAW

Edited by the
FACULTY OF POLITICAL SCIENCE
OF COLUMBIA UNIVERSITY

NUMBER 525

CREDIT UNION DEVELOPMENT IN WISCONSIN

BY

ELI SHAPIRO

CREDIT UNION DEVELOPMENT IN WISCONSIN

BY

ELI SHAPIRO

AMS PRESS
NEW YORK

COLUMBIA UNIVERSITY
STUDIES IN THE
SOCIAL SCIENCES

525

The Series was formerly known as
Studies in History, Economics and Public Law.

Reprinted with the permission of Columbia University Press
From the edition of 1947, New York
First AMS EDITION published 1968
Manufactured in the United States of America

Library of Congress Catalogue Card Number: 70-76652

AMS PRESS, INC.
NEW YORK, N. Y. 10003

To

MY MOTHER

AND

FATHER

AUTHOR'S PREFACE

In 1938 the Financial Research Program of the National Bureau of Economic Research undertook studies of three of the four principal cash credit lenders, namely, Personal Finance Companies, Personal Loan Departments of Commercial Banks and Industrial Banking Companies. These studies were published in response to the marked general interest in consumer credit which existed at the time. However, the fourth lender—credit unions—was not included in the series and the author, who was then on the staff of the Financial Research Program, subsequently decided to cover this fourth area independently.

Information was meager and fragmentary and what did exist was biased, written either by credit union promoters or by their competitors, representatives of commercial lenders.[1] No detailed analytical treatment of credit union statistics had been made and there was a recognized need for an exposition of the growth and operations of these institutions.

Since it was not practicable for a single author to conduct a national survey it was concluded that one state, with a credit union movement of sufficient magnitude to permit some generalizations, should be chosen.

In the final analysis this study was motivated by a desire to see to what extent credit union growth could be encouraged. A good deal of attention has been devoted to operational procedures and how they have been affected by the Statutes and by the State Banking Commission's rulings; lessons for administrators have been pointed out where it has seemed pertinent.

The author is indebted to many people for their part in making this study possible. Dr. Ralph A. Young, Director of the Financial Research Program of the National Bureau of Eco-

1 After 1938 some of these shortcomings were met by the publication of two books in the field, viz., J. L. Snider, *Credit Unions in Massachusetts* (Cambridge, 1939) and F. E. Wilcox, "A Statistical Study of Credit Unions in New York," *The Journal of Business of the University of Chicago*, Studies in Business Administration, vol. X, No. 2 (January, 1939).

nomic Research, first suggested a study of credit unions applying the techniques employed at the National Bureau of Economic Research in examining other consumer credit agencies. His constant encouragement and critical analysis in its various stages have made the finished product better than it would otherwise have been.

Miss Margaret Grobben, formerly economist for the Consumer Credit Institute of America, called attention to the credit union movement in Wisconsin and made available her private files and her knowledge of the subject matter. Without the practical experience and good judgment offered by Mr. Emmett G. Hampton, Credit Union Supervisor of the Wisconsin State Banking Department and Mr. J. Deanne Gannon, Acting Supervisor, this manuscript would never have been completed. These men gave unstintingly of their free nights and vacations to ensure completion of the work. Mr. J. Orrin Shipe, Mr. Charles Hyland, and Mr. Earl Rentfro of the Credit Union National Association cooperated by granting the all too many requests for data and for the results of their experience in the credit union movement. Miss Frieda Baird, formerly with the Credit Union Division of the Farm Credit Administration, examined parts of the manuscript and offered valuable suggestions as did Dr. Rolf Nugent of the Russell Sage Foundation.

To my faculty advisers, Professors H. S. Ellis, B. H. Beckhart and C. S. Shoup I am grateful for their suggestions and criticisms in reviewing the manuscript.

Mr. Victor Baxt, my student assistant, did the tedious work of computation in a most efficient manner and also made suggestions which are incorporated in the text. I am indebted beyond words to my sister, Miss Clara Shapiro, for her patience, skill and unselfish sacrifice of time in typing and improving the style of the manuscript, and to Mr. Donald Dunham who edited the final draft and put it into form for publication.

ELI SHAPIRO

TABLE OF CONTENTS

LIST OF TABLES

INTRODUCTORY STATEMENT

Credit unions are cooperative financial associations, corporate in structure, whose functions are to extend short-term cash credit at nominal rates of interest to their members and to promote thrift among them.[1] These associations have grown up in various parts of the country to meet the demands of low-income groups for small amounts of cash frequently for emergency purposes.

There are two types of credit unions—" open " in which membership is formed among the residents of a well-defined community and " closed " in which the members have a common employer or belong to the same fraternal, religious or other social or economic organization.

The working funds of the credit union are furnished chiefly through the sale of low denomination shares to its members. Payment can be made in instalments and dividends are declared out of earnings. When necessary, additional funds may be obtained by borrowing from outside sources, which normally means a bank or another credit union.

Rates of interest on loans are limited by Statute and the operations of a credit union are subject to the supervision of the State Banking Commission. Credit unions may also be established under the terms of the Federal Credit Union Act, administered by the Farm Credit Administration of the Department of Agriculture (now Federal Deposit Insurance Corp.) [2]

The credit union is filling a need for consumer credit of the low-income borrowers that is only partly met by the three major institutions in the field: personal finance companies, personal loan departments of commercial banks and industrial banking companies. It is supplying small sums of money needed for "necessitous" purposes to individuals at low rates of interest.

1 See Appendix I for a description of a typical Wisconsin credit union.

2 To date no credit unions have been incorporated under federal jurisdiction in Wisconsin.

By the end of 1939 there were 8,224 credit unions in the United States and they had $110,800,000[3] in loans outstanding on which 1 percent or less interest per month on unpaid balances was being charged.

Personal loan departments of commercial banks in 1939 were extending loans at the lowest rates of interest but were not prepared to make small loans to low-income borrowers. One explanation for this position was that commercial banks were venturing into what was to them a new field and were therefore extremely conservative in their loan practices.[4]

At the opposite extreme personal finance (small loan) companies made loans up to the statutory limit of $300 but were charging from 2 to 3 percent per month on unpaid balances. This charge was high in view of the borrower's income but so was the cost of operating and profits were not excessive.[5] Industrial banks at the same time were operating to meet credit demands of the middle income groups; their interest charges were scaled between those levied by personal finance companies and personal loan departments of commercial banks.

In this same period credit unions were lending at rates about one-half those charged by personal finance companies and their expenses were considerably lower. Nevertheless, like most cooperative ventures credit unions were slow in starting. The

3 United States Department of Commerce, Bureau of Foreign and Domestic Commerce, *Survey of Current Business*, September, 1941, p. S-13.

4 For further substantiation see J. M. Chapman, *Commercial Banks and Consumer Instalment Credit*, National Bureau of Economic Research (New York, 1940), p. 66; R. J. Saulnier, *Industrial Banking Companies and Their Credit Practices*, National Bureau of Economic Research (New York, 1940), p. 88, and R. A. Young, *et al.*, *Personal Finance Companies and Their Credit Practices*, National Bureau of Economic Research (New York, 1939), pp. 55-57.

5 These lenders are not to be confused with "loan sharks" who exact rates from 120 to 480 percent per annum and thrive particularly well in those states where personal finance companies are not permitted to operate.

initial inertia was due to the mystical aura with which the public surrounds finance. Prospective members were hesitant about placing their money at the disposal of financial novices and they themselves felt unqualified to serve on the credit committee which passes on applications for loans, as they might be required to do as credit union members.

These organizational difficulties obstructed the growth of credit unions. In 1934 the Credit Union Section of the Farm Credit Administration was established. Due to its promotional activities 3,452 federal credit unions were organized from 1934 until 1939 in comparison with 2,715 state credit unions in the country at large where promotion in each state except Wisconsin was not extensive.

However even this federal agency does not provide all the assistance needed and a strong case can be made for added help from state governments, as well as from the federal government, in the formation of credit unions and in extending supervision, examination and advice as required. The precedent for government assistance on an even wider scale than this anticipates already exists in the field of agricultural credit. In fact, in this field the government performs the role of commercial lender. Similar circumstances prevail in urban real estate financing, small business financing, and others. This proposed program would not be so costly nor involve so wide a departure from the traditional attitude of government not to interfere in business as other policies now being pursued.

It is not intended to imply that credit unions will eventually eliminate all commercial lenders from the market to which they cater. However, it is the author's impression that they will continue to make progressively greater inroads on the business. There are many prospective credit union members today obtaining loans from the more expensive sources who could be brought into unions if the states where they reside would follow the examples in promotion set by Wisconsin and by the federal government. With more adequate supervision and advice the number of credit union liquidations could be curtailed and thus one of the chief obstacles to membership would be removed. A detailed examination of the procedures instituted by Wisconsin may serve as a stimulus to other states and offer basic information which would prove valuable to them in establishing credit unions and expanding membership.

SUMMARY

WISCONSIN was one state which anticipated federal action in the promotion and organization of credit unions. By the end of 1939 this state ranked third among all states in the number of credit unions in existence and was the only state with no federal credit unions. Wisconsin made great strides in stimulating credit unions as is evidenced by the fact that it ranked first among all states in the number of organizations per 100,000 of total population. Excluding Nebraska, which had a unique type of credit union, Wisconsin also had the largest number of credit unions per 100,000 of urban population. However, the average resources per credit union in Wisconsin were smaller than for all credit unions in the country. By measuring credit union resources per $100,000,000 of income payments, variations in economic activity among the states was excluded and it was found that Wisconsin ranked third among the states.

The first credit union Statute in Wisconsin was passed in 1913 but no credit unions were organized until 1923 when the Legislature revised the Statute and made it more effective. From then until 1931 only 52 unions were chartered and finally the state authorities decided to take a direct hand in their promotion. A professional credit union organizer was put on the state payroll and the number of credit unions jumped to 563 by the end of 1939. Their total resources amounted to $9,300,000. Individual organizations ranged in size from several hundred dollars to over $300,000 depending mainly upon the number of years they have been in existence. Of the 563 credit unions in Wisconsin at the end of 1939 only 2 percent were " open " membership while 17 percent were the " closed " type formed by fraternal, religious or other social or economic organizations. Occupational unions also of the " closed " variety wherein the members have a common employer comprised the remaining 81 percent and were found particularly in the main industries of the state: food products, machine manufactures and paper.

For the end of 1939 Wisconsin credit union balance sheets showed that assets consisted mainly of loans to members and liabilities were composed mainly of members' shareholdings. Personal loans outstanding accounted for 70.7 percent, mortgage loans for 6.7 percent and investments for 7.5 percent of total assets. Members' shares outstanding together with dividend reserves and dividends credited to shares accounted for 92.2 percent of total liabilities, while the guaranty fund and undivided profit account comprised respectively 5.0 and 2.1 percent of liabilities. The older unions had a larger proportion of total assets invested in mortgage loans and a somewhat smaller cash account than the newer unions. The only marked difference in liabilities was that older unions had a proportionately larger guaranty fund account.

The ratio of borrowers to members rose from 36 percent in 1931 to 52 percent in 1936, thereafter fell to 45 percent in 1939. Average borrowers per credit union reached a new high of 106 in 1939. " Old " credit unions (chartered on or before December 31, 1932) had a higher ratio of borrowers to members than did " new " organizations. By 1939, 91 percent of all loans outstanding were personal loans as compared with 43 percent in 1932. The average size of credit union loans outstanding in 1931 was about $127—approximately the same average size as personal finance company loans outstanding. Thereafter it fell sharply, reaching a low of $61 in 1934 compared with $102 for personal finance companies. By 1939 the difference had diminished and was $110 for credit unions and $117 for personal finance companies. Judged by security for loans credit unions were characterized by co-maker endorsements and personal finance companies by chattel mortgages against personal property. However, this difference was rapidly diminishing. In 1931, 90 percent of credit union loans were endorsed by co-makers, but by 1939, only 47 percent were so secured while mortgages against personal property as security for loans had increased. In 1939, personal finance companies were still typified by loans secured by chattel mortgages against household furnishings; 80 percent of their loans were so secured. Losses on personal loans made were low; about .1 of 1 percent of volume of personal loans made have been lost. It would appear from this that credit union lending practice has been too conservative. The typical rate charged on credit union loans has been 1 percent per month on unpaid balances—approximately 75 percent of the credit unions charged this rate in 1939.

Credit unions are permitted to extend mortgage loans under the Wisconsin Credit Union Statute. However, the Banking Commission has sought to control and discourage this practice. Mortgage loans outstanding, which were 46.5 percent of personal loans outstanding in 1931 had fallen to 8.6 percent in 1939. About 53 percent of the loans made were over $2,000; 20 percent of the loans had a maturity of 24 months or less; 94 percent of the loans were made at the rate of 6 percent per annum or less. Compared with all credit unions in Wisconsin in 1939, credit unions extending mortgage loans were older, larger, had a larger potential membership, higher ratio of actual to potential members and also a higher ratio of borrowers to members. For the period 1929-1939 losses on mortgage loans were .16 of 1 percent of total mortgage loans made.

At the close of 1939, Wisconsin credit unions held investments in securities amounting to $694,302, of which 55.5 percent were in U. S. government bonds, 38.1 percent were in "other securities," while the remainder consisted of investments in municipal securities. In 1933, after a number of credit unions experienced difficulties with their investment, the Statute was revised to enable closer Banking Commission control over investments. Investments in common and preferred stock were practically eliminated and investments were restricted to class A, AA, or AAA corporate bonds. Compared with all credit unions, the organizations having investments in securities were older, larger, had a larger potential membership and a higher ratio of actual to potential members. There was no noticeable difference between these organizations and all credit unions with respect to the ratio of borrowers to members. From 1929 to 1939, $5,614 were charged to the guaranty fund as losses on investments. The highest losses occurred in 1935 and they were equal to 1.37 percent of investments outstanding in that year.

The ratio of total to potential membership in Wisconsin credit unions increased steadily from 1931 to 1939, reaching a new high of 41.7 in the latter year. Average membership per credit union also reached a new high—237.1 in 1939. Shareholdings per member which fell from a high of $95.18 in 1931 to a low of $44.62 in 1934 continued to rise thereafter attaining a figure of $64.09 in 1939. Dividends declared in 1939 were equal to 3.8 percent of all shares outstanding at the end of that year. Almost three-fourths of all credit unions paid dividends of 4 percent or more and the modal rate fell between 4.00 and 4.99. The " old " credit unions paid higher dividends than did the " new " credit unions.

It is generally recognized that operating expenses of credit unions are low especially when compared with commercial lending agencies. In 1939 expenses were 3.3 percent of average loans outstanding. The major component of expenses was salaries, followed by other expenses, interest on notes payable, rent and commissions. Gross earnings were 10.8 percent of average loans outstanding in 1939. Interest on loans accounted for 96 percent of all earnings while entrance fees, fines, or other fees, premiums on loans and profits on withdrawals account for the remaining 4 percent of income. Smaller credit unions are less efficient than larger ones but beyond the size of $2,500 in assets there is no evidence to indicate any optimum size of operation.

Credit unions are corporate organizations. In order to terminate their legal existence it is necessary to cancel their charter. The act of charter cancellation is known as liquidation. From 1923 through June 30, 1940 a total of 91 credit unions were liquidated—representing 13 percent of the total number organized in this period. 50 percent of the liquidations were due to lack of interest among actual or potential members, 14 percent were due to poor management, while 23 percent occurred because of a depression in the plant where the credit union was established. About 83 percent of all unions liquidating were 4 years old or less. It would appear that a Banking Department supervisor should be readily available to help newly formed credit unions over their initial difficulties; this would lower the mortality rate among young organizations. Only 17 percent of the liquidating credit unions had assets of $701 or over. Before a credit union is chartered, the Banking Department should examine the application carefully to determine whether or not the organization will attain a reasonable size. Should the prospect be dubious, the charter should not be granted. " Open " credit unions had the highest mortality rate among credit unions, classified by type of membership. Associational credit unions fared better than " open " organizations but had a poorer record than occupational organizations. The worst record among the associational credit unions was that of trade union organizations, followed by parish credit unions. While 10 percent of the occupational credit unions were liquidated, those organizations formed by state and federal employes and teachers showed no liquidations at all.

21.3 percent of all liquidating credit unions paid 79.9 percent or less of the amounts due shareholders. Around 19 percent of the liquidating organizations paid shareholders between 80 and 99.9 percent of the amounts due them. Approximately 60 percent of the liquidated organizations paid shareholders 100 percent or more of the amounts due them. The total amount of loss to shareholders in the cases of credit unions not returning 100 percent to shareholders was $956.78. However where liquidating organizations returned 100 percent or more of the amounts due shareholders, the total surplus over amount due was $3,150.08.

CHAPTER I

GEOGRAPHICAL DISTRIBUTION OF CREDIT UNION FACILITIES IN THE UNITED STATES, 1939

RURAL credit reform was included in the platform of all political parties in the presidential campaign of 1912. This emphasis upon farm aid was an attempt to placate the farm groups who disapproved of the Canadian reciprocity agreement. President Taft ordered the American ambassadors to various European nations to investigate the methods, institutions, and status of agricultural credit in these countries and the State Department issued a series of articles on " the European Co-operative system which was studied at the request of President Taft who wants to introduce a similar system in the United States." [1]

Mr. Myron T. Herrick, our Ambassador to France, made a very comprehensive study of cooperative systems for extending credit to farmers and concluded, " If American farmers had an organized system of mutual credit societies, they would save millions of dollars (in interest)."

On October 11, 1912, President Taft gave publicity to a letter which he had written to the governors of the various states, submitting Herrick's report and recommendation and urging the states to pass comparable legislation.[2] At the time this letter was circulated only one state, Massachusetts, had such legislation.[3] The year following Taft's letter, three states passed credit

1 H. B. Needham, "Easy Money for Farmers," *Country Gentleman*, Dec. 7, 1912.

2 The text of the President's letter to the states reads as follows: "A very good law has been enacted by the State of Massachusetts allowing the incorporation of credit unions which should furnish an example for other states. Their establishment is generally a matter of state legislation and encouragement, their organization and management wonderfully simple and their success is practically inevitable when the environment is congenial and where proper laws are passed for their conduct."

3 M. R. Neifeld, *Cooperative Consumer Credit* (New York, 1936), p. 30.

union laws, followed by one state in 1914 and four in 1915.[4]

The passage of enabling legislation merely makes the formation of credit unions legally possible. It does nothing to assist the development of a strong credit union movement. However, the government can render invaluable aid to the credit union movement in two ways. By making provision for a credit union organizer it can greatly facilitate the formation of a sufficient number of organizations. Furthermore once credit unions have been organized the government should exercise supervisory control over their financial operations, using the Banking Department (or another governmental agency) to provide advice, assistance, supervision including examinations, and generally point the way to sound financial practices.

The role of a professional organizer in promoting credit unions or any other form of cooperative cannot be over-emphasized. A major difficulty that seems to obtain in the cooperative movement is the lack of people who are ready to sacrifice the requisite time and effort necessary to " sell " the idea of cooperatives to potential members. The absence of a satisfactory promotional agency associated with the various credit union chartering bodies was a serious impediment to the strong development of credit unions in this country prior to 1934 (with the exception of Wisconsin since 1931). To substantiate this contention, one need only look to the tremendous strides made by credit unions since June 1934, which in major part, is the result of the administrative and promotional functions performed by the Farm Credit Administration's Credit Union Section. From June 1934 through December 31, 1939, 3,452 federal organizations were chartered and 3,074[5] of these reported outstanding loans of about 35.9 million dollars at the end of the period. At the end of 1939 the outstanding loans of federal credit unions alone were about one and one-third times as large

4 *Ibid.*, p. 30.

5 United States Department of Labor, Bureau of Labor Statistics, *Monthly Labor Review*, September, 1940, p. 657.

TABLE 1

GEOGRAPHICAL DISTRIBUTION OF CREDIT UNIONS IN THE UNITED STATES, DECEMBER 31, 1939[a]

State	State	Federal	Total	Total Pop.[b]	Urban Pop.[c]	Credit Unions per 100,000 Total Popul.	Credit Unions per 100,000 Urban Popul.
Alabama	65	20	85	2,832,961	855,941	.3	9.9
Arizona	4	17	21	499,261	173,981	4.2	12.4
Arkansas	21	15	36	1,949,387	431,910	1.9	8.4
California	157	248	405	6,407,387	4,902,265	5.9	8.3
Colorado	54	51	105	1,123,296	590,756	9.5	17.5
Connecticut		165	165	1,709,242	1,158,162	9.7	14.2
Delaware		12	12	266,505	139,432	4.0	8.6
Dist. of Col.	25	89	114	663,091	663,091	16.3	17.3
Florida	42	100	142	1,897,414	1,045,781	7.5	13.5
Georgia	89	37	126	3,123,723	1,073,808	4.1	11.8
Idaho		30	30	524,873	176,708	6.0	16.7
Illinois	574	97	671	7,897,241	5,809,650	8.5	11.5
Indiana	146	145	291	3,427,796	1,887,712	8.6	15.3
Iowa	205	5	210	2,548,268	1,084,231	8.4	19.1
Kansas	77	19	96	1,801,028	753,941	5.3	12.8
Kentucky	94	9	103	2,845,627	849,327	3.7	12.1
Louisiana	25	77	102	2,363,880	980,439	4.3	11.1
Maine	3	33	36	847,226	343,957	4.5	10.6
Maryland	34	27	61	1,821,244	1,080,351	3.4	5.1
Massachusetts	402	73	475	4,316,721	3,859,476	11.0	12.2
Michigan	165	66	231	5,256,106	3,454,867	4.4	6.6
Minnesota	324	14	338	2,792,300	1,390,098	12.1	24.1
Mississippi	7	13	20	2,183,796	432,882	.9	5.0
Missouri	325	26	351	3,784,664	1,960,696	9.2	17.2
Montana	8	16	24	559,456	211,535	4.0	12.0
Nebraska	159	27	186	1,315,834	514,148	14.3	37.2
Nevada		4	4	110,247	43,291	4.0	2.9
New Hampshire	8	6	14	491,524	283,225	2.8	4.7
New Jersey	50	166	216	4,160,165	3,394,773	5.1	6.4
New Mexico		11	11	531,818	176,401	2.2	5.5
New York	184	458	642	13,479,142	11,165,893	4.8	5.8
North Carolina	112	31	143	3,571,623	974,175	4.0	14.3
North Dakota		37	37	641,935	131,923	6.2	28.5
Ohio	276	219	495	6,907,612	4,612,986	7.2	10.8
Oklahoma	45	37	82	2,336,434	879,663	3.6	9.1

TABLE 1 *continued*

State	State	Federal	Total	Total Pop.[b]	Urban Pop.[c]	Credit Unions per 100,000 Total Popul.	Credit Unions per 100,000 Urban Popul.
Oregon	30	37	67	1,089,684	531,675	6.1	13.4
Pennsylvania	77	438	515	9,900,180	6,586,877	5.2	7.8
Rhode Island	18	15	33	713,346	653,383	4.7	5.1
South Carolina		33	33	1,899,804	466,111	1.7	7.0
South Dakota		18	18	642,961	158,087	3.0	11.3
Tennessee	67	63	130	2,915,841	1,027,206	4.5	12.6
Texas	87	253	340	6,414,824	2,911,389	5.3	11.7
Utah	28	22	50	550,310	305,493	9.2	16.7
Vermont		5	5	354,231	123,239	1.3	4.2
Virginia	30	65	95	2,677,793	944,675	3.5	10.1
Washington	145	43	188	1,736,191	912,969	11.1	20.4
West Virginia	18	43	61	1,901,974	534,292	3.2	11.5
Wisconsin	563		563	3,137,587	1,679,144	18.2	33.1
Wyoming		17	17	250,742	93,527	.8	18.9
TOTAL	4,743	3,452	8,195	131,669,275	74,423,702	6.2	11.0

SOURCE: United States Department of Labor. Bureau of Labor Statistics, *Monthly Labor Review,* September 1940, p. 656.

[a] The total number of credit unions estimated by the Bureau of Labor Statistics is 8,315 which does not include a few unchartered organizations estimated at not more that 25 for which no data are available since they formed before the passage of credit union legislation in their states. The total revised number is 8,195 since the 91 organizations in Hawaii, 20 state chartered organizations in Iowa (7 chartered but not yet in operation, 13 in voluntary liquidation), 8 state chartered associations in Minnesota which are also in voluntary liquidations and 1 federal credit union which has been chartered to operate in Wisconsin but had not been in operation are excluded.

[b] Rather than use an intercensal estimate for the population of the United States in 1939, the population figures for 1940 as reported by the Bureau of the Census are employed. See United States Department of Commerce, Bureau of the Census, *Sixteenth Census of the United States: 1940.*

[c] The urban population is composed mainly of persons living in incorporated places (cities, towns, villages, or boroughs) having a population of 2,500 or more. In addition, a few townships, not incorporated as municipalities but having a population of 10,000 or more and a population density of 1,000 or more per square mile, were classified as urban, and finally a special rule was applied to the towns in New Hampshire, Massachusetts and Rhode Island under which an entire town (township) was counted as urban if it contained a village having a population of more than 2,500 and forming more than one-half of the total population of the town, *ibid.*

as the outstandings of all credit unions in existence in the United States at the end of 1933.[6]

Table I shows the geographical distribution of credit unions as of December 31, 1939. The total number of credit unions per state (including the District of Columbia as a state) varied from a low of 4 in Nevada to a high of 671 for Illinois. The state with the next highest number of credit unions was New York with 642 associations, while Wisconsin ranked third among all states in 1939 with 563 credit unions. The only other state with over 500 credit unions was Pennsylvania, which had 515.

In 1937 the Bureau of Labor Statistics' estimates of credit unions as of the end of that year [7] placed Wisconsin at the top of the list with a total of 488 credit unions; Illinois was next with 481, while New York and Massachusetts followed with 449 and 415 respectively. In the two years elapsing since the end of 1937, Wisconsin no longer had the largest total number of credit unions, having been exceeded by both Illinois and New York.

Ten states, Connecticut, Delaware, Idaho, Nevada, New Mexico, North Dakota, South Carolina, South Dakota, Vermont and Wyoming, had no state-chartered credit unions at the end of 1939. However, only one state, Wisconsin, had no federal credit unions.

One reason for the absence of federal chartered unions in Wisconsin lies in the paternalistic attitude of the state government toward cooperatives. By employing a credit union promoter in 1931, this state had anticipated the Credit Union Division of the Farm Credit Administration by about three years. The latter organization was established with a view to supplying promotional, administrative and advisory functions

6 *Federal Reserve Bulletin*, April, 1943, p. 344.

7 U. S. Department of Labor, Bureau of Labor Statistics, *Monthly Labor Review*, October, 1938, pp. 802-803.

in those states where credit union legislation made no provisions for these services. Since the state of Wisconsin was performing more or less of these functions, in its credit union legislation, the Farm Credit Administration did not actively push its promotional work in that state. After the passage of the Federal Credit Union legislation in June of 1934, one federal organization was chartered in Wisconsin but it never did any business. Since its initial entrance into Wisconsin, the Farm Credit Administration has apparently avoided competition with the state Banking Department in the matter of chartering credit unions. It is believed that a tacit agreement between the state Banking Department and the Farm Credit Administration whereby the latter has not engaged in active promotional work in Wisconsin explains the absence of federal credit unions in the state.

Another reason why prospective credit unions in Wisconsin have not taken out a federal charter is to be found in the less stringent provisions in the state law regarding credit union operations. For example, the organizations chartered by the state of Wisconsin can extend real estate loans which they would not be permitted to do under the federal Statute. This provision is apparently of some importance to Wisconsin credit unions since at the end of 1939 they had $622,069 worth of outstanding mortgage loans which accounted for about 6.5 percent of their total assets.

A more significant measure of the distribution of credit unions in the United States than the absolute numbers is the number of organizations per 100,000 of population. It is here that one sees the strides which Wisconsin has made in encouraging and stimulating the growth of a large number of small credit unions. Wisconsin had the largest number of credit unions per 100,000 of population (18.2). The nearest competitor was the District of Columbia with 16.3 credit unions per 100,000 population, while Nebraska, Minnesota, Washington and

Massachusetts followed in that order with 14.3, 12.1, 11.1, and 11.0 credit unions per 100,000 population.

Of the three states most famous for the large number of credit unions, namely Massachusetts, New York and Illinois, New York had 4.8 credit unions per 100,000 population, Illinois, 8.5 and Massachusetts, 11.0. It would appear therefore, that on a comparable basis Wisconsin had a more highly developed credit union movement than any other state in our country.

It could be argued that the use of total population as the denominator, for testing the prevalence of credit unions, distorts the resultant conclusions since the credit union is primarily an urban phenomenon. An examination of the type of membership of Wisconsin credit unions in 1939, shows that 81 percent of the number are in industrial (urban) plants. Of the associational credit unions, only 4.1 percent are formed among farm cooperatives and some of the "other" cooperatives are undoubtedly located in rural areas; most of the associational credit unions derive their membership from urban areas. The remaining 2 percent are community credit unions, some of which are also located in urban areas.

Further substantiation of the assertion that the credit union is essentially an urban phenomenon is afforded by an examination of the Bureau of Labor Statistics' estimates of credit unions classified by type of membership at the end of 1936.[8] Of the 4,034 organizations reporting, 37 were composed of employees of farm organizations, 130 drew their membership from a specified locality, while 97 had their membership in residents of a specified locality and members of a specified religious sect or church. One hundred and twenty-four had no restrictions of any kind placed upon their membership. The 37 farm organizations were clearly located in rural areas but it is difficult to say

8 Florence E. Parker, *Consumers' Cooperation in the United States, 1936*, p. 122. United States Department of Labor, Bureau of Labor Statistics (Bulletin No. 659).

how many of the others were located in rural localities. Some of them were, but the precise number is purely conjectural. Even assuming that all these unions were found in rural areas, they would only comprise 10 percent of the total.

In order to get a more adequate measure of the density of credit unions, the rural population has been excluded from the total population, giving figures for urban population by states. The number of credit unions per 100,000 of urban population was then compiled. Nebraska showed the largest number of credit unions per 100,000 of urban population, with 37.2. However, that state has shown evidence of development of a unique type of credit union. Since the banking holiday and subsequent bank closings, the state has many rural areas that have no commercial banks because the closed institutions have not been permitted to reopen or have not been reopened. To fill the void in these bankless communities, many cooperative associations which are called credit unions have been chartered by the Banking Department to engage in what is more correctly considered commercial banking rather than credit union business. Thus the number of credit unions in Nebraska has been greatly exaggerated.[9]

Next to Nebraska, Wisconsin showed the largest number of credit unions, 33.1 per 100,000 of urban population. The nearest to Wisconsin in the matter of associations per 100,000 of urban population is North Dakota with 28.5, followed by Minnesota, Washington, Iowa and Wyoming with 24.1, 20.4, 19.1 and 18.9 respectively. Massachusetts, Illinois, Pennsylvania and New York, states famous for their credit union development, show up relatively poorly. Massachusetts leads with 12.2 per 100,000 of urban population, followed by Illinois, Pennsylvania and New York which have 11.5, 7.8 and 5.8 respectively.

9 Lincoln Clark, "Credit Union Legal Framework," Part II, *The Journal of Business of the University of Chicago,* January, 1944, vol. XVII, No. 1, p. 59.

TABLE 2

STATE AND FEDERAL—CHARTERED CREDIT UNIONS IN THE UNITED STATES AND IN WISCONSIN, DECEMBER 31, 1939

	Credit Unions			Total Assets of Unions		
	Number	Percent of United States or Wisconsin Total	Wisconsin as a percent of United States Totals	Amount of Assets	Percent United States or Wisconsin Total	Wisconsin as a percent of United States Total
United States	8195	100.0		$191,231,862	100.0	
State Charter	4743	57.9		145,803,444	76.2	
Federal Charter	3452	42.1		45,428,418	23.8	
Wisconsin	563	100.0	6.8	9,287,975	100.0	4.9
State Charter	563	100.0	6.8	9,287,975	100.0	4.9
Federal Charter	—	—	—	—	—	—

SOURCE: United States Department of Labor, Bureau of Labor Statistics, *Monthly Labor Review* September 1940, p. 656, for estimated number of credit unions in the United States. See footnote a, p. 28, for revision of this number. The figures for total resources of credit unions in the United States is taken from *Monthly Labor Review, op. cit.*, p. 659. There is a discrepancy between the number of credit unions in existence and the number of organizations reporting resources. The latter figures cover 7,751 credit unions of which 4,677 are state chartered and 3,074 are federal chartered. This sum covers 95 percent of the number of credit unions estimated in the country.

Of the estimated 8,195 active credit unions in the United States at the end of 1939, 58 percent were state-chartered and accounted for 76 percent of total resources [10] while 42 percent of the organization had federal charters and accounted for only 24 percent of total resources (Table 2).

10 If the number of credit unions reporting assets is used, 57 percent of the number were state chartered and accounted for 76 percent of the resources while the remaining 42 percent were federal chartered and accounted for 24 percent of the resources.

Of the number of credit unions in the United States 6.8 percent were located in Wisconsin. However, these organizations accounted for only 4.9 percent of the total resources in the country. Since the data on resources include only 7,751 organizations, the Wisconsin unions comprised 7.3 percent of the number reporting assets and accounted for only 4.9 percent of total assets. It would appear that Wisconsin had successfully promoted a large number of small credit unions.

The fact that the average credit union in Wisconsin had less resources than the average for the United States is not necessarily indicative of overzealous promotion of small credit unions. For example, the plants in Wisconsin may be smaller than the average for the country so that one would expect fewer resources per credit union.

It was desired to find the relative importance of credit union resources to total economic activity and Table 3 was compiled showing credit union assets per $100,000,000 of income payments for all states.[11]

For the country as a whole in 1939 credit unions had $270,866 of assets per $100 million of income payments. Massachusetts led all states with $789,216 of credit union resources per $100 million of income payments, followed by Rhode Island with $762,791 and Wisconsin which had $615,092. Vermont had the smallest volume of credit union assets, $3,294 per $100 million of income payments.

Thus while the average resources per credit union in Wisconsin were smaller than the average for the United States, when the volume of economic activity per state is introduced, Wisconsin ranked high judged by the volume of assets accumulated by its credit unions.

11 Income payments were chosen as the best single measure of economic activity.

TABLE 3

GEOGRAPHICAL DISTRIBUTION OF CREDIT UNION RESOURCES IN THE UNITED STATES, DECEMBER 31, 1939

State	Total Resources	Income Payments (in millions)	Resources per $100,000,000 Income Payments
Alabama	$ 1,413,319	$ 681	$207,838
Arizona	197,741	227	89,863
Arkansas	236,235	478	50,255
California	14,599,521	5,047	289,672
Colorado	1,800,319	563	321,482
Connecticut	2,453,720	1,301	188,746
Delaware	85,704	203	42,850
District of Columbia	4,522,193	813	565,262
Florida	1,944,380	819	243,037
Georgia	3,096,774	901	344,077
Idaho	125.271	213	62,600
Illinois	21,688,582	5,285	410,766
Indiana	4,213,778	1,688	250,820
Iowa	3,076,440	1,185	260,711
Kansas	1,248,433	692	180,927
Kentucky	2,381,094	839	286,867
Louisiana	1,778,945	828	216,939
Maine	590,231	400	147,550
Maryland	1,325,831	1,074	123,906
Massachusetts	24,465.707	3,106	789,216
Michigan	7,463,161	3,054	244,691
Minnesota	7,440,423	1,378	543,094
Mississippi	249,694	436	58,046
Missouri	7,413,671	1,832	405,114
Montana	123.992	288	44,250
Nebraska	3,146,141	523	605,019
Nevada	10,879	84	13,500
New Hampshire	564,574	268	217,115
New Jersey	4,685,058	2,859	164,385
New Mexico	60,497	179	35,529
New York	20,438,066	11,301	180,867
North Carolina	1,522,676	1,090	139,688
North Dakota	154,980	209	77,450
Ohio	6,783,377	4,154	163,453
Oklahoma	1,000,541	796	126,645
Oregon	1,170,175	587	201,741
Pennsylvania	9,347,451	5,819	160,884

TABLE 3 *continued*

State	Total Resources	Income Payments (in millions)	Resources per $100,000,000 Income Payments
Rhode Island	$ 3,661,485	$ 480	$762,791
South Carolina	221,735	493	45,244
South Dakota	198,746	227	90,318
Tennessee	2,655,899	853	312,447
Texas	6,684,208	2,554	262,125
Utah	699,064	243	291,250
Vermont	5,613	174	3,294
Virginia	1,647,514	996	166,414
Washington	2,584,613	1,012	255,900
West Virginia	692.947	714	97,591
Wisconsin	9,287,975	1,514	615,092
Wyoming	72,516	141	51,785
TOTAL	191,231,862	70,601	270,866

SOURCE: Resources taken from United States Department of Labor, Bureau of Labor Statistics, *Monthly Labor Review*, September 1940, p. 659. Income payments taken from United States Department of Commerce, *Survey of Current Business*, August 1945, p. 17.

CHAPTER II

GROWTH, SIZE AND TYPES OF MEMBERSHIP OF WISCONSIN CREDIT UNIONS

GROWTH OF WISCONSIN CREDIT UNIONS

IN 1913 Wisconsin enacted a credit union law but no organizations were established. Under the 1913 law no provisions were made for methods of raising funds, methods of lending, types of loans, administration or investments. Answers to these specific problems were essential to the organization of credit unions and no action could be taken until they were clarified. Furthermore there was no active promotion of credit unions in the state. In 1922 the Credit Union National Extension Bureau[1] ventured into Wisconsin to achieve passage of adequate credit union legislation and to promote credit unions after the legislation was enacted. Satisfactory legislation was passed in 1923 when the Statute was revised and the enabling provisions for credit unions were placed under the Building and Loan Statutes. Also, the duties and responsibilities of credit union officers were more carefully defined; unsecured loans were limited to a maximum of $50; surplus credit union funds could be invested in securities that were legal investments for building and loan associations. Almost immediately after the passage of the new law, the municipal employees in Milwaukee organized the first credit union in the state and by the end of 1923 there were two organizations with resources totaling $3,600.

Formation of credit unions under the new law proceeded very slowly. By the end of 1926 there were still only two organizations, but their resources had increased to $78,400. Beginning in 1927 there was a slow but steady increase in the number of

1 Organized in 1921 by Mr. Edward A. Filene, a Boston business man and philanthropist, to achieve adequate credit union legislation in the various states and to promote organization of credit unions until they were more popular and well known.

organizations and an almost comparable growth in resources which continued through 1930 when there were twenty-two unions with resources of almost a half million dollars. When new credit unions are chartered they are invariably small and as the number of organizations increases without a comparable rise in assets the average resources per credit union fall.

The year 1931 represents the beginning of a new era in the Wisconsin credit union movement, principally due to a change in attitude by the state government toward these cooperative credit associations. The Statutes with regard to credit unions were revised to include the following provisions:

> It shall be the duty of the (State) Banking Department to promote the extension of credit at the lowest possible rates and cooperate with every group of people who may be, or may become, interested in the formation and development of a credit union in this state for that purpose, and it shall have authority to do all things reasonably necessary for the discharge of this duty. The Banking Department shall carry on advertising of whatever character is most suitable and effective to acquaint the people of this state with the agencies and organizations dealing in consumer credit and of the rates of interest, the conditions of loans, the benefits and safeguards and the saving features of each type, agency and organization.[2]

The state appropriated $5,000 to permit the appointment of a credit union organizer attached to the Building and Loan Division of the Banking Department which at that time was charged with supervision of credit unions.[3] His duty was to travel around the state and speak at various plants, parishes, townships or any other places where it was possible to promote a credit union. Despite the fact that he started his organizing campaign in the middle of the depression of the 1930's a sharp rise took place in the number of unions as may be seen in Table

2 Laws of Wisconsin Chapter 186, Paragraph 186.21.

3 Subsequently raised to $7,500.

4. By the end of 1933 there were 201 unions; resources had more than doubled during the period 1930-33 and amounted to approximately $1,100,000.

TABLE 4

NUMBER AND RESOURCES OF WISCONSIN CREDIT UNIONS
DECEMBER 31, 1923 THROUGH DECEMBER 31, 1939

Year	No. of of Unions Reporting	Total Resources	Average Resources per Credit Union
1923	2	$ 3,600	$ 1,800
1924	2	29,500	14,750
1925	2	53,800	26,900
1926	2	78,400	39,200
1927	6	129,000	21,500
1928	10	202,200	20,220
1929	13	328,000	25,230
1930	22	481,900	21,904
1931	52	669,100	12,867
1932	132	888,700	6.732
1933	201	1,094,000	5,442
1934	277	1,790,100	6,462
1935	383	2,914,400	7,609
1936	455	4,582,500	10,071
1937	488	6,407,600	13,130
1938	542	7,426,700	13,702
1939	563	$9,287,900	$16,497

SOURCE: Files of Wisconsin State Banking Department.

The growth of credit unions was the result also of the interest and encouragement shown by the credit union section of the state Banking Department.[4] The administration at that time even went so far as to assume that credit unions could fill the needs of all Wisconsin citizens for consumer credit. At the fall session of the State Legislature in 1931, Lieutenant Governor Huber is reported to have asked for the repeal of the small loan

4 *Bridge*, Christmas issue, 1933, " Wisconsin Credit Union Growth."

law and the substitution of the credit union idea under the aegis of the Banking Department.[5]

The rapid growth of credit unions continued and by the end of 1938 there were 542 unions representing a 230 percent increase over 1933. Over this same period resources increased about 700 percent. In 1938 the credit union promoter was removed from the state payroll for the sake of economy and the organization of credit unions in the state was taken over by the Credit Union National Association and the Wisconsin Credit Union League with its local organizations. By the end of 1939 there were 563 chartered credit unions with resources of approximately $9,287,000.

TABLE 5

LOANS OUTSTANDING IN CREDIT UNIONS, PERSONAL FINANCE COMPANIES AND INDUSTRIAL BANKS IN THE UNITED STATES AND WISCONSIN, DECEMBER 31, 1939

Institution	United States		Wisconsin	
	Loans Outstanding	Percent of Total	Loans Outstanding	Percent of Total
Credit union	$189,200,000	21	$ 7,197,900	23
Personal finance company	434,500,000	49	6,904,700	21
Industrial bank ...	256,600,000	30	17,676,000	66
	$880,300,000	100	$31,778,600	100

SOURCE: Department of Commerce, Bureau of Domestic and Foreign Commerce *Survey of Current Business*, April 1941, for United States totals. Files of Wisconsin State Banking Department for Credit Union totals. *Annual Report of Small Loan Companies for 1939*, State of Wisconsin Banking Department for Personal Finance Companies. Data for Industrial Banks was supplied by Mr. Rolf Nugent, Director of Consumer Credit Studies, Russell Sage Foundation, New York.

5 *Capital Times* (Madison, Wisconsin), December 22, 1931.

Credit Unions and Other Consumer Finance Institutions in Wisconsin

Table 5 establishes a comparison between the distribution of consumer credit loans outstanding of cash credit lenders in the United States and Wisconsin. While credit unions accounted for 21 percent of outstanding loans in the United States, they supplied 23 percent of the consumer credit business in Wisconsin. Personal finance companies fared far worse in Wisconsin than they did in the country at large, accounting for only 21 percent of the state's business but about 50 percent of the country's business. Industrial banks had a far greater share of the state's consumer credit business—66 percent—than they did for the country.[6]

It is interesting to observe how rapid had been the rate of growth of credit union loans in Wisconsin compared with those of other agencies (Figure 1). While there is no evidence to indicate that credit unions have seriously displaced other types of personal loan agencies, it does appear that if their growth continues as in the past they will obtain a greater share of the personal loan business and may even slow down the growth of some commercial agencies that compete most directly with them.

Size of Wisconsin Credit Unions

A distribution of credit unions by size of assets is given in Table 6. In 1932, around 74 percent of the total number of unions had assets under $2,500; by 1934, 64 percent were in this category, but by the end of 1939 only about 30 percent of the number of unions owned under $2,500. While in 1932 about two-fifths of the organizations had assets of less than $500, in 1934 one-fifth fell into this category and by the end of 1939

6 While there are four major types of institutions to which individuals desiring to make personal loans may resort, personal loan departments of commercial banks were excluded since it was impossible to obtain data on outstanding loans for Wisconsin. For that reason they were also excluded from the national totals.

FIGURE 1

LOANS OUTSTANDING, WISCONSIN 1929-1939

Credit Unions Personal Finance Companies Industrial Banking Companies

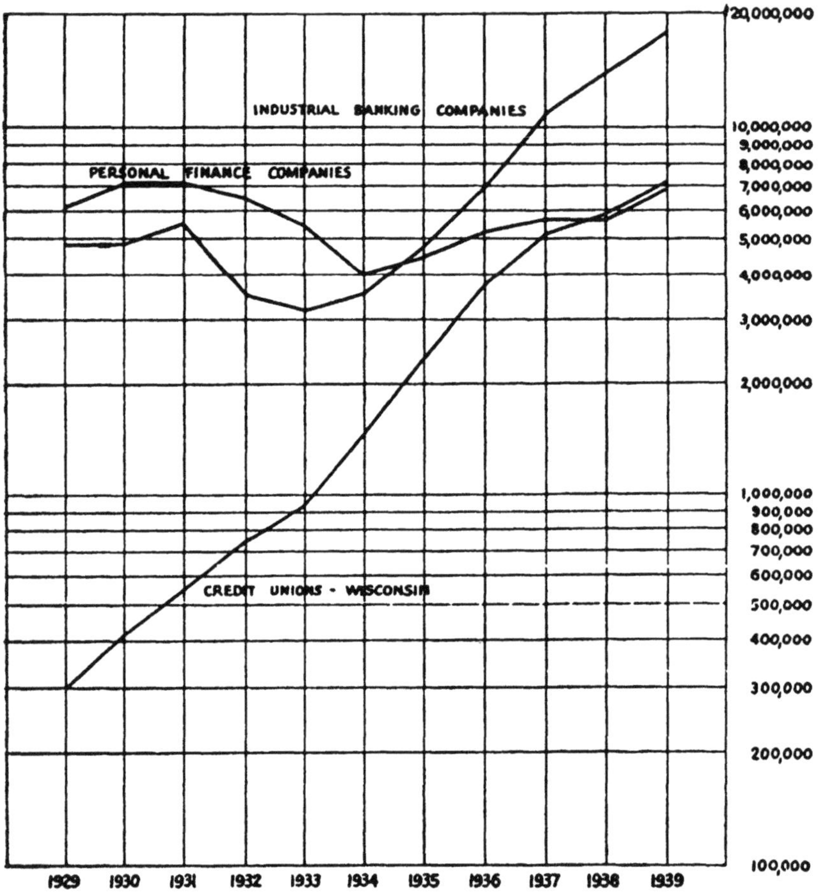

TABLE 6

WISCONSIN CREDIT UNIONS CLASSIFIED BY SIZE OF ASSETS
1932, 1934 AND 1939

	December 31, 1932		December 31, 1934		December 31, 1939	
Total Assets	Number	Percent	Number	Percent	Number	Percent
Less than $500	55	41.9	57	20.6	58	10.3
$500 - $999	16	12.2	37	13.4	31	5.3
$1,000 - $2,499	26	19.8	84	30.3	77	13.7
$2,500 - $4,999	13	9.9	43	15.5	104	18.5
$5,000 - $9,999	5	3.8	25	9.0	101	17.9
$10,000 - $14,999	5	3.8	12	4.3	63	11.2
$15,000 - $24,999	1	.7	5	1.8	56	9.9
$25,000 - $49,999	..	..	6	2.2	41	7.3
$50,000 - $99,999	1	.7	2	.7	16	2.8
$100,000 - $249,999 ...	2	1.5	1	.4	12	2.1
$250,000 - $499,999 ...	1	.7	1	.4	3	.5
$500,000 - and over ..	..	..	..	..	1	.3
No business	6	4.5	4	1.4	..	..
TOTAL	131	100.0	277	100.0	563	100.0

SOURCE: Files of Wisconsin State Banking Department.

only one-tenth were in this group. The percentage of credit unions falling into the $500 to $999.99 category remained about 13 percent in 1932 and 1934 and fell to around 5 percent in 1939. Unions in the category of $1,000 to $2,499.99 in assets comprised about 20 percent of the total in 1932, about 30 percent in 1934 and around 14 percent at the end of 1939. Over this same period there was a steady increase in the percentage of unions found in the $2,500 to $5,000 range, rising from 10 percent in 1932 to around 19 percent by 1939. The tendency for unions with large assets to multiply over the period 1932 through 1939 is clearly seen for organizations with assets under $250,000. However, unions having assets in excess of $250,000 remained roughly the same.

TABLE 7

"NEW" AND "OLD" CREDIT UNIONS CLASSIFIED BY SIZE OF ASSETS ON DECEMBER 31, 1939[a]

Total Assets	"New" Credit Unions		"Old" Credit Unions	
	Number	Percent	Number	Percent
Less than $500	56	12.2	2	1.9
$500 - $999.99	27	5.9	4	3.8
$1,000 - $2,499.99	68	14.8	9	8.7
$2,500 - $4,999.99	88	19.2	16	15.4
$5,000 - $9,999.99	82	17.9	19	18.3
$10,000 - $14,999.99	44	9.6	19	18.3
$15,000 - $24,999.99	41	8.9	15	14.4
$25,000 - $99,999.99	41	8.9	16	15.4
$100,000 - $249,999.99	10	2.2	2	1.9
$250,000 and over	2	.4	2	1.9
TOTAL	459	100.0	104	100.0

SOURCE: Files of Wisconsin State Banking Department.

[a] "New" credit unions include all organizations chartered *on January 1, 1933 or thereafter.* "Old" credit unions cover any organization chartered *on or before December 31, 1932.*

In order to test the relationship between size and age of a credit union, a frequency distribution of size of unions was broken down into two separate categories (Table 7). The first consists of " new " unions, which had been chartered from January 1, 1933 through December 31, 1939 and were in existence six years or less. " Old " unions comprise organizations chartered on or before December 31, 1932, which have therefore operated anywhere from seven to seventeen years.

Twelve percent of the " new " unions had assets under $500 while only 2 percent of the " old " unions fell in this category. Eighteen percent of the " new " unions had assets under $1,000 as against only 5.7 percent of the " old " unions. In fact, for each class interval up to $5,000, the " new " unions contribute a higher percentage of the total than do the " old " unions. Each class interval beginning with assets of $5,000 or more showed a greater frequency of occurrence among " older " than among " newer " organizations. About 19 percent of the " old " organizations have assets of $25,000 or more while only about 11.5 percent of the " new " institutions fell in this size group.

The correlation between age and size is most apparent in the earlier years although it holds true for the later years as well (See Appendix II). None of the 43 unions that were less than 1 year old had assets in excess of $10,000 while 11 percent of the unions one year old fell into this size category. For older organizations, the percentage of unions with assets in excess of $10,000 increases steadily until we come to the six year old organizations, where the proportion reaches 65 percent. For seven and eight year old organizations, the percentage declines: about 45 percent of these unions have assets in excess of $10,000. Another rise is registered for nine year old institutions where roughly three-fourths fall in the over $10,000 category while in ten and over ten year old organizations, 100 percent of the total belong in this category.

While it seems fairly clear that in a general way the size of a credit union, measured by total assets, is related to its age, there are other factors which affect size as well. The size of the town, the size of the plant, or the income of its members plays a part in determining size. Homogeneity of potential membership may also affect size. To illustrate, in a community with a mixture of Polish, German and Dutch descendants, friction developed when Germany invaded Poland and the Low Countries. The differences that arose tended to keep the size of credit unions down. Adequacy of management also plays its part in determining and maintaining membership.

Type of Membership

One of the principles which evolved out of the experience of the " Rochdale Society of Equitable Pioneers " established in England in 1844 was the extension of democracy in the co-operative movement by permitting unlimited membership. Anyone may join a cooperative with the sole proviso that only those persons who might harm the society by using it for purposes of individual advantage can be prevented from joining [7]. By the very nature of credit union operations the aforementioned tenet of Rochdale cooperation has to be modified in order to insure the safety of loans made, the accuracy and honesty with which funds are handled, and to assure a mutuality of interest among members known to one another and therefore in a position to judge the trustworthiness of those who apply for loans and those who run the credit union.

Therefore, the Statutes under which credit unions operate usually require that the organization shall only include certain individuals as members. These credit unions have a "closed" type of membership which is formed among persons having some common bond of employment, religious faith, association, etc., which provides enough common affinity of interest to cement the members together. Membership is limited to persons within that group and all trustworthy persons may join the organization. The "closed" credit unions can be broken down into two major sub-types; one known as the associational, and the other as the occupational, or as it is sometimes called, the industrial or employee type.

Credit unions of the associational type of membership consist of persons who belong to a specific labor union, cooperative, religious, professional, fraternal or other organization. In the occupational type, all the members are drawn from persons working in the same plant, in the same store, or in the same government bureau, etc.

There are some organizations which can be described as "open" credit unions. Their members are not bound together by strong common interests. Usually the common denominator in the "open" credit union resides almost exclusively in the fact that the membership lives in a specified community or

7 See James P. Warbasse: "Basic Principles of Cooperation," *Annals*, American Academy of Political and Social Sciences, May, 1937, pp. 7-16.

group of communities. As of December 31, 1939 there were only eleven such unions or 2 percent of the total number. While this is a very small percentage, it is biased downward. It is difficult to find the exact amount because there are some credit unions in Wisconsin, organized in rural communities that practically do have " open " charters. The membership clause in these organizations usually reads " any member or patron of such and such cooperative organization," and the bond is usually weak because almost everyone in the community is considered as a member of the cooperative organization. However, the understatement is estimated to be very small.

The credit union division of the Banking Department discourages the formation of " open " charter credit unions because in large communities the lack of personal relationships on the part of the members of an " open " type union frequently leads to a loosely-knit organization in which the management may easily become careless or even dishonest. Further, the members are usually disinterested and the safety of the funds may become impaired. In Wisconsin there are a few " open " credit unions which are organized to encompass several small towns where there are not enough members to form a union in one community. Such unions labor under a dual handicap: there are the usual disadvantages of heterogeneous unions to which are added the distances between the towns which increase the impersonality and apathy. That these disadvantages are significant will be brought out in a later chapter on liquidations of credit unions.

At the end of 1939, the occupational type of union was the most common. 455 unions, or 81 percent of the total number were of the employee category; these unions are spread over a variety of industries (Table 8). The type of industry in which credit unions exist reflects principally the major types of industry found in the state. Plants engaging in machine manufactures and in paper manufactures, two of Wisconsin's leading industries, show the largest number of credit unions in the

TABLE 8

CLASSIFICATION OF WISCONSIN CREDIT UNIONS BY TYPE OF MEMBERSHIP, DECEMBER 31, 1939

Types of Membership	Number	Percent of Total
Associational—"Closed"		
Farm Cooperatives	23	4.1
Other Cooperatives	32	5.7
Religious	25	4.4
Labor Unions	14	2.5
Fraternal and Professional	2	.3
Sub Total	96	17.0
Occupational—"Closed"		
Automotive Products	16	2.8
Banking and Insurance	9	1.6
Beverages	4	.7
Construction and Materials	1	.2
Educational		
Colleges	4	.7
Schools	12	2.1
Electric Products	3	.5
Food Products		
Bakery, grocery & produce	5	.9
Dairy	22	3.9
Meat packing	8	1.4
Other	3	.5
Furniture	5	.9
Government		
Federal	27	4.8
State	13	2.3
County	5	.9
Local	23	4.1
Hardware	3	.5
Hotels and Restaurants	2	.4
Laundries and Cleaners	5	.9
Leather	12	2.1
Machine Manufactures	43	7.7
Metals and Foundries	27	4.8
Paper	41	7.3
Petroleum	5	.9
Printing and Publishing		
Newspapers	16	2.8
Others	10	1.8

TABLE 8 *continued*

Types of Membership	Number	Percent of Total
Public Utilities		
Heat, light and power	21	3.7
Telegraph and Telephone	9	1.6
Rubber	2	.4
Trade (Merchandising)	20	3.6
Textiles and Hosiery	9	1.6
Transportation		
Bus and Truck	7	1.2
Railroad	20	3.6
Miscellaneous Manufactures	43	7.7
Sub Total	455	81.0
Residential—" Open "		
Community	11	2.0
Sub Total	11	2.0
GRAND TOTAL	562	100.0

SOURCE: Files of Wisconsin State Banking Department.

employee type of organization. Organizations in the metal industry and foundries each supply about 5 percent of the number of unions. Representation among government employees is unequal. Federal employees supply about 5 percent of the organizations, local government employees about 4 percent, state employees about 2 percent, with less than 1 percent among county government employees. About 4 percent of the total number of unions are organized in the dairy industry, one of Wisconsin's leading industries. A number of varying industries each supply over 2 percent of the number of credit unions.

Approximately 17 percent of the total number of unions were of the associational type of membership. Almost 10 percent of the number were organized among cooperatives; about 4 percent were farm cooperatives while the remainder consisted of other types of cooperatives. This relatively heavy representation among cooperatives is due to the heavy concentration of cooperatives in Wisconsin. Religious credit unions are also popular, comprising about 4.5 percent of the total number of organizations. These are formed almost exclusively among the parishes of the Catholic Church. The remainder of the associational credit unions is found among labor unions (2.5 percent) and fraternal and professional groups.

CHAPTER III

ANALYSIS OF ASSETS AND LIABILITIES

In 1930 the twenty-two reporting credit unions showed on their balance sheets that personal loans to members accounted for one-half their assets, mortgage loans one-third, while the remainder consisted of investments (10 percent) and cash (4 percent).

By the end of 1933, the relative distribution of assets for the 201 reporting credit unions did not show much change as compared with the end of 1930. Loans to members fell slightly to 48 percent while mortgage loans rose to 36 percent of total assets. Investments fell to 8 percent and the cash account rose to 7 percent over this period. The depression did not cause a decreased demand for funds in Wisconsin as was the case for the country.[1] One reason for this may be that the credit union movement was just getting under way in Wisconsin and the addition of new unions led to an increase in the demand for loan facilities of these organizations, thus keeping the loan figure from falling.

As a result of the continued expansion of the credit union business, and also the improvement of general business conditions in the period following 1933, there was a marked increase in the personal loan account by the end of 1939. Seventy percent of the assets of the 563 reporting unions consisted of loans to members, representing an increase of over twenty percent as compared with 1933. While the proportion of assets consisting of loans to members had been increasing, the proportion of mortgage loans to total assets decreased precipitously. (Table 9).

In the early thirties the credit unions more nearly approximated building and loan associations than organizations purporting to care for the consumer credit needs of low income

1 *Federal Reserve Bulletin*, April, 1943, p. 344; also F. E. Wilcox, *op. cit.*, p. 31, for the New York State experience.

TABLE 9

ASSETS AND LIABILITIES OF ALL WISCONSIN CREDIT UNIONS AS OF DECEMBER 31, 1930, 1933, AND 1939.

Item	1930 Amount	1930 Percent of Assets	1933 Amount	1933 Percent of Assets	1939 Amount	1939 Percent of Assets
Number of Unions	22		201		563	
ASSETS						
Loans to members	$248,301	51.5	$530,449	48.5	$6,569,031	70.7
Mortgage loans	168,085	34.9	393,809	36.0	622,069	6.7
Loans to other unions	—	—	—	—	6,850	.1
Investments	45,592	9.5	91,243	8.3	694,303	7.5
Cash and due from banks	19,173	4.0	77,437	7.1	1,332,446	14.3
Real Estate owned	—	—	—	—	23,961	.3
Furniture & Fixtures	261	.0	203	.0	13,874	.1
Other Assets	548	.1	931	.1	25,441	.3
TOTAL ASSETS	481,960	100.0	1,094,960	100.0	9,287,975	100.0
LIABILITIES						
Shares	421,934	87.5	966,944	88.4	8,286,708	89.2
Dividends credited on shares	15,407	3.2	17,021	1.6	251,145	2.8
Reserve dividends pay.	697	.1	1,946	.2	19,548	.2
SUB TOTAL	438,038	90.8	985,911	90.2	8,557,401	92.2
Guaranty Fund Res.	16,612	3.5	48,146	4.4	465,965	5.0
Undivided profits	13,316	2.8	30,155	2.8	198,182	2.1
Notes payable	9,900	2.1	26,755	2.4	32,762	.4
Other reserves	—	—	2,715	.2	29,442	.3
Other liabilities	4,094	.8	390	.0	4,223	.0
TOTAL LIABILITIES	481,960	100.0	1,094,072	100.0	9,287,975	100.0

SOURCE: Files of Wisconsin State Banking Department.

borrowers, since over a third of their assets consisted of loans against real estate. Early in 1934, however, the Wisconsin Banking Commission became dissatisfied with this mortgage lending business and the Commission has since that time pursued a policy of minimizing it.[2] The Commission's success is apparent from Table 9 which shows that by the end of 1939 only seven percent of the assets of all reporting unions consisted of mortgage loans; a decrease of about thirty percent since 1933.

At the end of 1939 investments declined slightly as compared with 1933, and accounted for 7.5 percent of all assets. However, the cash account continued to rise and reached a figure of 14 percent of all assets. The growth of the cash account, which represents a non-earning asset against which dividends must be paid, has caused concern to the credit unions and they have in some instances tried to remedy this by limiting shareholdings.

The liabilities of all the credit unions reporting consist mainly of members' shareholdings. At the end of 1930 approximately 91 percent of the total liabilities consisted of shareholders' contributions. These contributions consisted chiefly of shares outstanding (87.5 percent) while dividends credited to shares (3.2 percent) and reserve for dividends payable at a later date (.1 percent) account for the total sum. Members' shareholdings remained practically constant in 1933 and by the end of 1939 rose slightly so that it was equal to about 92 percent of all liabilities.

The Wisconsin statute until 1941 required that the credit union set up a guaranty fund to meet contingencies or losses in its business.[3] Before paying a dividend, each union had to set aside to this fund twenty percent of its net income accumulated during the fiscal year until the fund equaled ten percent

2 See pp. 88 ff. for a more extended treatment of mortgage loans.

3 Wisconsin Statutes, Chapter 108, Section 186.17.

of total assets. When the fund fell below this ten percent level, annual contributions amounting to 20 percent of net income were required to build it up to the statutory figure. Upon recommendation of the board of directors, the members may, at their annual meeting, increase, or if the fund equals or exceeds the amount of capital stock paid in, decrease the proportion of profits required by the statute to be set aside. In 1930 this fund for all credit unions reporting was equal to 3.5 percent of total liabilities; by the end of 1933 it had risen to 4.4 percent and in 1939 reached a new high of 5.0 percent. As the number of credit unions reaches a plateau the ratio of older unions to all unions would increase and the older unions would have a larger guaranty fund than new unions because they have had a longer time to accumulate a guaranty fund. It is reasonable to expect that the guaranty fund will therefore increase over the years.[4]

The Wisconsin statute pertaining to credit unions makes no reference to the establishment of an undivided profits account. Sound financial practice would require the establishment of a separate account to serve as a buffer against unforeseen contingencies which may arise. Instead of distributing all their earnings in large dividends, credit unions are following a more conservative policy of paying a dividend sufficiently high to encourage thrift among their members and are setting aside the surplus in the undivided profit account. When this account is set up, losses and other unexpected expenses can be deducted without having to dip into the guaranty fund. Furthermore, by

4 In the 1941 session of the legislature, Section 186.17 of the statute was amended in order to give the Banking Commission more discretionary control over the guaranty fund. The major feature of the revised statute is the provision for the setting aside to the guaranty fund of at least 20 percent of net income before paying dividends. Twenty percent is now the minimum, not the maximum and can be increased by the Commission when the fund is less than ten percent of assets; the Commission can also order the transfer of any reserves and undivided earnings to the fund when it falls below the stated 10 percent. The provision in the old statute that the guaranty fund should be accumulated until it equals or exceeds the amount of capital stock actually paid in is omitted in the new law.

building up their surplus account credit unions are developing a reserve from which they can draw in order to maintain a uniform dividend rate in the event that earnings are decreased at some later period. The undivided profit account amounted to 2.8 percent of total liabilities at the end of both 1930 and 1933 and by the end of 1939 it had fallen to 2.1 percent. This decrease is the result of the policy instituted in the late thirties by the Banking Department which required that a greater portion of earnings be set aside in the guaranty fund. In many cases credit unions were ordered to transfer their entire undivided profits account to the guaranty fund. The reason the control office has insisted upon this is to give the shareholding members greater protection on their investment in the credit union. Once the funds are transferred to the guaranty fund they can be used for only protective purposes.

Thus there has been a slow but steady increase in the guaranty fund and the undivided profits account taken together. These accounts are the first to be drawn upon in the event of loss and the ratio of their total to outstanding loan balances is significant. In 1930 the combined amounts of the guaranty fund and undivided profits account of Wisconsin credit unions was equal to 7.2 percent of all loans outstanding; by 1933 it had risen to 8.5 percent and in 1939 it was equal to 9.2 percent. Consequently by increasing reserves against losses and unforeseen contingencies they found themselves in a stronger financial position in 1939 than in 1930. A comparison of this same ratio on December 31, 1939 for the 102 credit unions chartered on or before December 31, 1932 and all organizations shows that the older unions had a ratio of 11.8 as contrasted with 9.2 for all credit unions. It is of course to be expected that the older unions would by virtue of their longer existence have had greater opportunity to strengthen their financial status.

The large proportion of funds supplied by their own shareholders in the main is ample for their purposes and therefore Wisconsin credit unions like most credit unions under normal conditions have not had to borrow large sums of money from outsiders. The exception occurs when there is a sudden increase in loan demands; they are then forced to resort to commercial banks for funds. Repayments are made from new shareholders'

TABLE 10

ASSETS AND LIABILITIES AS OF DECEMBER 31, 1939 OF 102 WISCONSIN CREDIT UNIONS OPENED ON OR BEFORE DECEMBER 31, 1932.

Item	Amount	Percent of total
ASSETS		
Loans to members	$1,556,039	65.0
Mortgage Loans	379,006	15.8
Loans to other unions	1,350	.1
Investments	166,191	6.9
Cash	267,705	11.2
Other Assets	24,278	1.0
TOTAL	$2,394,569	100.0
LIABILITIES		
Shares	$2,125,598	88.0
Reserves for dividends payable	4,073	2.0
SUB TOTAL	2,129,671	90.0
Guaranty fund	170,842	7.1
Undivided profits	57,976	2.4
Notes payable	8,455	.4
Other reserves	27,328	1.1
Other Liabilities	297	.0
TOTAL	$2,394,569	100.0

SOURCE: Files of Wisconsin State Banking Department.

investments as they come in.[5] Notes payable, which represent outside borrowing were equal to about 2.0 percent at the end of 1930, and rose to about 2.5 at the end of 1933 as a result

5 Section 186.11 of the statute regulating credit unions provides that an organization may borrow money not to exceed 25 percent of the total assets for temporary purposes. The board of directors may borrow this money for a period of ninety days unless the Commissioner of Banking approves an extension of time. These loans shall be made only if the available cash is insufficient to make loans approved by the credit committee or if the request for withdrawal exceeds available cash.

of the generally chaotic financial conditions prevailing in the early part of that year. By the end of 1939 they fell to less than .5 percent of total liabilities since contributions by shareholders more than covered the current demand for loans.

The older credit unions—chartered on or before December 31, 1932—have a smaller proportion of their assets outstanding in loans to members than do all unions, 65 percent as against 71 percent (See Tables 9 and 10). Another marked difference between old and all credit unions is the relatively high proportion of total assets that consist of mortgage loans in the former group. Sixteen percent of the total assets of the 102 old credit unions was invested in mortgage loans while the proportion for all credit unions was only 4 percent. Most of the younger unions were so small that they were prohibited by law from making real estate loans, while the older and larger unions found mortgage investments more lucrative with the easy money rates during the thirties than investments in securities.

The cash item accounts for about 11 percent of total assets in the old credit unions which is somewhat smaller than for all unions where it amounts to 14 percent. One reason for this may be the reluctance of the newer unions to place their surplus funds in the low-yield securities open to them for investment since they anticipate a possible increase in the demand for loans in the near future. It is found that investments for all unions are insignificantly higher than for the old unions.

A comparison of the liabilities of the old and all credit unions shows a fairly close relationship except for the guaranty fund account. This item comprised 5.0 percent of the liabilities of all unions in contrast to 7.13 percent for the old unions. Since the fund is built up over a period of time from net earnings, it is reasonable to expect older organizations to have developed a large guaranty fund.

CHAPTER IV

LOANS TO MEMBERS

THE Statutes pertaining to credit union operations [1] and the model by-laws supplied to credit unions set the *modus operandi* of loan practice in Wisconsin. Both the by-laws and the Statute expressly state that the capital and surplus funds of the credit union shall be lent to members in good standing for provident purposes. Loans are made only to members and a member borrower must have at least one share of fully-paid stock in order [2] to be eligible.

The personal loan function is the primary objective of the credit unions. Deposits in banks, mortgage loans and investments are to be resorted to *only* if the organization has funds in excess of its needs for making personal loans. All loans in excess of $50 must be secured by such collateral as the credit committee shall approve or shall be guaranteed by one or more persons whose responsibility is acceptable to the committee. The credit unions objected to the small sum of the unsecured loans they could make since members had to obtain co-makers if they wanted to borrow sums in excess of $50. Obtaining of co-makers was irksome to borrowers who resented having to ask their fellow workers or friends and relatives to serve as co-makers for their loans since they had to divulge their personal financial status to these people and frequently friendships and cordial relationships were broken up when a prospective co-signer was reluctant or refused to sign a note. It was argued that many members of credit unions were not using the loan facilities of their organizations but were instead utilizing other and higher cost cash lenders since the added cost was considered less burdensome than the psychic cost of obtaining a co-signer. The per-

1 Chapter 186 Sections 186.9 and 186.11.

2 With the exception of a few older organizations which may lend to a member who has only partly paid stock.

sonal finance companies were freely utilized and they would lend up to $300 requiring only a chattel mortgage against property as security for the loan. As a result of the pressure brought by the credit unions on both the Banking Department and the State Legislature, the law was revised in 1935 to permit the board of directors or the credit committee, whenever they are of the unanimous opinion it is for the best interest of the credit union to make unsecured loans up to $100.[3]

There is a passage in the law which limits unsecured loans of $100 to borrowers whose " financial rating or assets are such as to assure the repayment of said loan ". This clause is obviously intended to stress the need for closer scrutiny by the credit committee of applications for $100 unsecured loans, and to underline the particular responsibility of the committee since their decision has to rest to a large extent on character rather than upon collateral.

While neither the Statutes nor the model by-laws specify the maximum or minimum maturity of a loan, the by-laws do state that the term of a loan " shall bear some relation to the amount involved and the circumstances of the borrower and shall be in conformity with such general regulations as may be laid down from time to time by the board of directors." The rate of interest charged on loans is determined from time to time by the board of directors and the maximum interest charge on loans shall be 1 percent per month on unpaid balances. A borrower may repay the whole or any part of his loan at any time. Credit unions' personal loans to an individual member are not limited

3 The credit unions were not satisfied with this provision and continued to fight to raise the maximum size of unsecured loans. One of the major grievances they held, judging by comments raised by credit union officials was that personal finance (small loan) companies could make unsecured loans up to $300. In the 1941 session of the Wisconsin legislature the statute was revised to permit credit unions to make unsecured loans up to $300. Before a union can make such a loan, however, it must apply to the Banking Department and be examined by that body which may grant or refuse that permission to the organization.

in size nor are they in any way related to the amount of his shareholdings.

The actual practice employed in applying for and in extending loans varies from credit union to credit union. There is enough uniformity of procedure, however, to present a general description which is based upon information supplied by the Banking Department, several credit union officials and the Credit Union National Association. An applicant for a loan must file his request in writing. The prospective borrower goes to the treasurer, fills out a loan application stating the amount of money desired, the purpose of the loan and the security for the loan, if any. The reverse side of the application provides for a résumé of the applicant's financial status. The information called for includes the following:

1. Bank loans outstanding
2. Other credit union loans outstanding
3. Other loans outstanding
4. Real estate and other property owned
5. Occupation
6. Weekly and monthly income
7. Bank accounts

Usually the same information is required for co-makers. Some credit unions require this material from all applicants while others merely ask it of new applicants. Under the model by-laws the credit union is given the power to declare any loan immediately due and payable if any of the facts are found to be misstated in the application or if the borrowed money has been used for purposes other than those stated in the application.

The application is given to the treasurer who turns it over to the credit committee. The credit committee must pass upon loan applications unless the prospective borrower is a member of that committee, in which case the application is referred to the board of directors. Applications must receive a unanimous approval before receiving their funds;[4] they may appeal from the decision

4 Changed to majority approval in 1941.

of the committee to the board of directors. The committee keeps a record of the proceedings and all applications for loans of $500 or more must be sent to the board of directors for their approval.

The credit committee is empowered to refuse any loan application unless it promises to be "of benefit to the borrower." To expedite the credit committee's action the treasurer, when submitting the application for a loan, usually attaches a brief résumé of the past credit experience of the applicant. Fundamentally, the decisions of the committee are based upon the past credit experience of the applicant, his character, the adequacy of the security and the borrower's needs. The application is returned to the treasurer when approved and the action is recorded and the money is given to the borrower by check or in cash.

In the early stage of a credit union's existence, the ratio of borrowers to total members is very low and tends to increase as the age of the organization increases (Table 11). At the outset an organization must accumulate funds from shareholders' investments which in turn are loaned to members. The growth of funds is usually much less rapid than the demand for loans and many prospective borrowers must be rejected. Furthermore, it is generally agreed that the market for consumer credit is imperfectly competitive.[5] Many persons out of habit, convenience and lack of knowledge of credit unions continue to use the higher cost commercial lenders although they are eligible to membership in a cooperative association which extends credit service at a lower cost. As the years pass, the share contributions of members increase, and therefore the number of borrowers that can be accommodated increases. As the credit union gets older, it may put on a drive to get more

5 Theodore O. Yntema, "The Market for Consumer Credit: A Case in 'Imperfect Competition,'" *Annals*, American Academy of Political and Social Science, March, 1938, pp. 79-85. R. A. Young and Associates, *op. cit.*, pp. 155-160.

borrowers or the potential borrowers may become aware of its existence and service, and use it instead of the commercial lender. Finally, it is quite likely that the initial membership of a credit union is composed largely of persons for whom the appeal of a credit union centers around the thrift motive.

In 1931, 36 percent of all credit union members were borrowers. Beginning with 1932, however, the credit union movement really gathered momentum in Wisconsin and the ratio rose to 45 percent. The low point, about 40 percent, was reached in 1933 and the high point, 52 percent in 1936. One reason why this ratio has not been higher has been the mushroom growth of credit unions in which the young organizations have a low ratio of borrowers to members, thus bringing down the figure for all institutions. The number of credit unions in Wisconsin appears to be reaching a plateau and it will be interesting to see what effect stability in the number of organizations will have upon the borrower to member ratio.

There are, of course, many other factors to be considered in determining the ratio of borrowers to members, such as the degree of competition from other cash credit lending agencies, the state of business generally and secular growth in consumer credit. Distrust of credit unions and higher returns on investments elsewhere are also factors which affect the number of people who join credit unions.

In order to discover the changes in number of borrowers being served by the credit unions from 1931 through 1939, the number of borrowers reported by all organizations at the end of the year was divided by the number of credit unions in existence which gives a figure for average number of borrowers per union. This figure is, of course, subject to the inherent disadvantages of any average. The average number of borrowers per credit union fell from 44 in 1931 to 34 in 1932. This decline is due to the fact that the real growth of credit unions starts in 1932 when the rate of growth in the number of credit unions exceeded that in borrowers so the average borrowers per union declined. Beginning with 1933 the increase in borrowers exceeded the rate of increase in number of unions so that average borrowers per credit union increased steadily and by 1939 the figure was 106 borrowers per credit union.

Ten percent of all credit unions had a ratio of borrowers to members in excess of 60 percent while 23 percent of the " old " unions fell into this group. It appears that the older unions have a greater frequency of borrowing members than all unions. About 18 percent of all unions had a borrower to member ratio of 30 percent or less while only 4 percent of the old unions were found in this category. We find that 37 and 34 percent of all unions fit into the 31 to 45 and 46 to 60 percent ratio of borrower to member class intervals respectively while the corresponding figures for old unions is 22 and 51 percent (Tables 12 and 13).

TABLE 11

MEMBERS AND BORROWERS IN WISCONSIN CREDIT UNIONS—1931-1939

Year Ending Dec. 31	Total Membership	Borrowing Members	Percent Borrowers to Members	Average Borrowers Per Union
1931	6,429	2,320	36.2	44.8
1932	10,136	4,519	44.5	34.2
1933	19,470	7,647	39.2	38.0
1934	37,236	16,046	43.0	57.9
1935	57,487	25,892	45.0	67.6
1936	80,284	41,734	51.9	91.7
1937	101,226	49,623	49.0	101.6
1938	117,423	52,715	44.8	97.2
1939	133,504	59,698	44.7	106.0

SOURCE: Files of Wisconsin State Banking Department.

TABLE 12

RATIO OF BORROWERS TO MEMBERS CLASSIFIED BY SIZE OF MEMBERS—
WISCONSIN CREDIT UNIONS, 1939

Actual Membership	Number of Organizations	Ratio of Borrowers to Members					
		1-15	16-30	31-45	46-60	61-75	Over 75
0 — 99	231	23	41	75	61	25	6
100 — 199	159	2	21	63	60	8	5
200 — 299	60		5	29	21	3	2
300 — 399	32		2	12	17	1	
400 — 499	21		4	8	8		1
500 — 599	8			1	5	2	
600 — 699	8			2	4	2	
700 — 799	4			2	2		
800 —and over	28			13	12	2	1
TOTAL	551	25	73	205	190	43	15

SOURCE: Files of Wisconsin State Banking Department.

TABLE 13

RATIO OF BORROWERS TO MEMBERS CLASSIFIED BY SIZE OF MEMBERS—
"OLD" CREDIT UNIONS, 1939

Actual Membership	Number of Organizations	Ratio of Borrowers to Members					
		1-15	16-30	31-45	46-60	61-75	Over 75
0 — 99	48	3		12	20	9	4
100 — 199	30		1	9	14	4	2
200 — 299	9			2	6	1	
300 — 399	4				4		
400 — 499	2			1	1		
500 — 599	3				2	1	
600 — 699	2				1	1	
700 — 799							
800 — and over	5				4	1	
TOTAL	103	3	1	24	52	17	6

SOURCE: Files of Wisconsin State Banking Department.

Personal loans comprised around 68 percent of all loans outstanding in 1929 but declined thereafter and reached a low of 43.5 in 1931 (Table 14). Beginning in 1932, they rose steadily every year and by the end of 1939 accounted for 91 percent of total loans. This increase is explained in part by the deliberate policy of the Banking Department to curtail the amount of money loaned by credit unions on mortgages against real estate. Since the outlet for funds in the mortgage loan field was reduced, credit unions had to hold idle cash, make investments or increase the volume of personal loans outstanding. Since the latter course was the most profitable there was a concerted drive by these organizations to get new borrowers. Furthermore, as the credit union gained in reputation as an established source of consumer credit, many eligible people who heretofore had failed to join became members. The change in the Statute relaxing the $50 maximum limit on unsecured loans also encouraged new borrowers to appear at the credit union rather than at other cash credit lending agencies. Finally, the upsurge in economic activity stimulated the demand for consumer credit and credit unions partook of this improvement.

The proportion of mortgage loans outstanding declined steadily during the period and in 1939 reached a low of 8.6 percent.[6] In 1938 there appears for the first time an item called loans to other credit unions. Prior to this year credit unions were prohibited from lending money to another credit union, under ruling by the Attorney General in which it was stated that a corporation cannot become a member of a credit union; hence one credit union cannot become a member of another credit union and therefore cannot qualify for a loan as a member.[7] On March 15, 1938, the Commissioners received a new ruling from the Attorney General in which the opinion was expressed that loans to other credit unions would count as part of the investment of

6 Mortgage loans are discussed at greater length on p. 88 ff.

7 24 Attorney General 223, May 10, 1935.

surplus funds permitted under section 186.11 of the statutes, providing that the approval of the Banking Department is obtained before the " investment " is made.[8] These loans are arranged through unsecured promissory notes running for ninety days.

In 1938 and 1939 credit unions made loans to other credit unions, although the amounts made were insignificant; in 1939 these loans amounted to $6,850.[9] The inter-credit union loans are usually negotiated between organizations located in a large town. The reason for this may be that these towns have local chapters of the Wisconsin Credit Union League at whose meetings officials of the various credit unions in the chapter can discuss their problems and thus borrower and lender are brought together.

In order to get some information on the type of borrowers served by small loan companies and credit unions the average size of loan outstanding was compiled for both institutions from 1931 through 1939 (Table 15). For small loan companies the total of outstanding loans at the end of the year was divided by the number of accounts outstanding, and for credit unions the total personal loans outstanding were divided by the total number of borrowers. A more accurate figure for average personal loans outstanding for credit unions would be a figure representing not total borrowers but borrowers of personal loans. However, it is not possible to break down the borrower figure by type, so the figure for total borrowers was used to give a rough

8 " It shall be lawful for the board of directors to borrow money not to exceed 25 percent of the total assets but not for a longer period than ninety days except that such period may be extended when approved by the Banking Commission."

9 In 1939 notes payable of credit unions amounted to $32,762. Despite the fact that the rate paid on bank loans is usually higher than the rate paid on loans from credit unions, bank loans are more popular since they can be obtained in a short time without red tape and without seeking the approval of the Banking Commission.

TABLE 14

PERCENTAGE DISTRIBUTION OF ALL LOANS OUTSTANDING AT END OF YEAR, CLASSIFIED BY TYPE, 1929-1939

Year	Total All Loans Outstanding	Percent of Total Loans: Personal Loans Outstanding	Mortgage Loans Outstanding	Outstanding Loans to Other Credit Unions	Total
1929	$293,486	67.8	32.2	—	100.0
1930	416,385	59.6	40.4	—	100.0
1931	552,887	43.5	46.5	—	100.0
1932	745,696	43.7	46.3	—	100.0
1933	924,257	57.4	42.6	—	100.0
1934	1,488,108	66.5	33.5	—	100.0
1935	2,377,567	77.5	22.5	—	100.0
1936	3,663,575	85.7	14.3	—	100.0
1937	5,157,454	90.3	9.7	—	100.0
1938	5,987,760	90.5	9.4	.1	100.0
1939	7,197,948	91.2	8.6	.2	100.0

SOURCE: Files of Wisconsin State Banking Department.

approximation of average personal loans outstanding. Since the number of mortgage loans was not very large in the later thirties, the distortion is not great. From 1931 to 1934 or 1935, however, mortgage loans were a much more important portion of total loans outstanding and the average personal loan outstanding for credit unions is distorted by appearing smaller than it would have been had only personal loan borrowers been included.

Another element of bias enters into the estimate of average size of credit union personal loans outstanding. One weakness of an arithmetic mean is the disproportionate weight it gives to extreme cases. Personal finance companies can make loans only up to $300. However, loans are fairly evenly distributed throughout the range of $1 to $300 so the average loan outstanding is not a greatly distorted figure. There is no maximum size of loan stated in the credit union statute or model by-laws and a number of loans in excess of $500 are made with the resultant range for loans much wider than in the case of personal finance companies. The existence of these loans in excess of $500 tends to distort upwards the average size of loans outstanding. As an offset is the fact that credit unions make many more small-sized loans ($25 and under) than do personal finance companies.[10] Thus there are factors in the loan practice of credit unions which tend to understate and overstate the average size of personal loans outstanding. Unfortunately no data are available to reach any conclusion about net distortion resulting from these opposing factors.

In 1931 the average size of credit union and small loan company loans outstanding was about the same. Beginning in 1932, both types of loan decreased steadily through 1934 but the average size for credit unions fell much more precipitously. In 1935 the average size of loan outstanding for both institutions began to increase and at the end of 1939 the figure was $110 and $117 respectively. Judged by the average size of loan outstanding on this latter date, credit unions and personal finance companies were servicing the same sort of borrowers.

By comparing the security behind credit union loans with that behind those of personal finance companies some light is thrown on the credit-extending practices of these agencies (Table 16). The most prevalent type of security for credit unions throughout the period 1931-39 was notes secured by endorsement of other members. There is no set practice followed by credit unions on the number of co-makers required for a loan, but normally there is one co-maker for each $100 loaned. One objectionable feature of this procedure lies in "round robin co-signing" which simply means that John Jones signs for John Smith and *vice versa*. If this practice becomes wide-

10 See R. A. Young and Associates, *op. cit.*, p. 46 for distribution of personal finance companies' loans by size.

spread the contingent liability piled up is so large that the co-maker feature is practically valueless as security for a loan. The credit committees attempt to cope with this problem by placing a ceiling on liability that may be incurred by a co-maker, by limiting it to a stated percent of the co-signer's income or by reporting the co-maker's contingent claims on the application blank of the loan which the borrower submits to the credit committee to pass upon.

In those unions which are subsidized in part by the plant as a gesture toward labor relations the ill-will engendered by compelling a co-maker to pay up on a defaulted loan frequently redounded to the embarrassment of the plant and thus defeated the objective of its gesture.

TABLE 15

AVERAGE SIZE OF LOAN OUTSTANDING CREDIT UNIONS AND PERSONAL FINANCE COMPANIES, 1931-1939

Year	Average Credit Union Personal Loan Outstanding	Average Personal Finance Company Loan Outstanding
1931	$126.91	$125.67
1932	88.64	113.54
1933	69.36	105.09
1934	61.66	101.81
1935	71.12	104.93
1936	75.21	111.16
1937	93.80	111.66
1938	102.84	109.65
1939	110.03	117.32

SOURCE: Data on credit unions compiled from files of Wisconsin Banking Department. Personal finance statistics from *Annual Report of Small Loan Companies* for 1939, State of Wisconsin Banking Department, p. 10.

Endorsement by members served as security for about 75 percent of all personal loans outstanding in 1931 and 1932, and then declined steadily so that by 1939 it comprised only 35 percent. The credit unions pursued a policy of requiring other types of security which was the result in part of their members' objections to co-maker notes.

In some cases the co-maker of a credit union loan is not a member of the credit union. Usually this type of endorsement is found where the member gets someone in his family to serve as endorser of his note. Also there is a growing number of cases involving " merchant debt readjustment ": a man in debt for instance to a local merchant or doctor induces the creditor to serve as co-maker, obtains a loan from his credit union, and turns the money over in payment of his debt. Endorsement by other than members served as security for 15 percent of all personal loans outstanding in 1931 and has declined steadily since then to about 10 percent.

In 1931 mortgages on personal property—usually on automobiles, household furniture, radios, and other forms of durable consumers' goods—were not an important form of security for credit union personal loans, comprising only 2.5 percent of all personal loans outstanding. This form of security, typically used by personal finance companies, increased rapidly during the thirties until it reached 27 percent of all outstanding personal loans by 1939. Credit union members objected strenuously to the requirement of co-signers for loans and pointed to the practices of the personal finance companies as preferable. More and more frequently the credit committees have had to yield to the weight of their argument and accept mortgages on personal property as security for loans. In fact some credit unions actually prefer definite collateral such as chattel mortgages to co-maker loans.

Some credit union members secure their loans by pledging their union shares as collateral. This form of security has never been very important and accounted only for 3.5 percent of all personal loans outstanding in 1939. At first glance it would appear short-sighted for a member to use his savings and to pay a higher rate of interest than he receives when his savings could be converted into cash. However, there are reasons why

TABLE 16

CREDIT UNION PERSONAL LOANS OUTSTANDING, YEAR ENDING 1931 THROUGH 1939 CLASSIFIED BY TYPE OF SECURITY

Type of Security	1931	1932	1933	1934	1935	1936	1937	1938	1939
Endorsement by members	75.1	74.2	63.5	57.3	50.5	42.7	40.9	38.4	36.2
Endorsement by other than members	15.4	13.4	14.1	11.8	12.4	10.4	10.3	11.1	10.7
Mortgages on personal property	2.5	2.7	3.7	5.8	10.4	18.3	22.8	22.7	26.9
Stocks and bonds	4.0	1.7	2.8	3.2	2.7	2.7	2.2	2.1	1.8
Assignment of shares	1.1	2.3	3.9	4.0	3.8	3.8	3.8	3.7	3.5
Other security	.7	1.7	1.3	4.3	5.0	5.6	8.5	8.4	7.5
Unsecured	1.2	4.0	10.7	13.6	15.2	16.5	13.6	13.6	13.4
TOTAL	100.0	100.0	100.0	100.0	100.0	100.0	100.0	100.0	100.0
Total Personal Loans Outstanding	$295,704	$400,599	$530,449	$989,442	$1,841,431	$3,130,907	$4,655,070	$5,421,328	$6,569,030

SOURCE: Files of Wisconsin State Banking Department.

this method of borrowing is not so short-sighted. If he needs money at the end of the period for which dividends are to be declared, he would stand to lose his entire dividend for that period by withdrawing his shares. Furthermore, some people find it impossible to save except under some form of compulsion; hence they prefer to keep their savings intact, and incur indebtedness to the credit union wherein the pressure to repay would be stronger than the incentive to accumulate savings.

Despite the early limit of unsecured loans to $50 the pressure upon the credit unions was so great that they made as many unsecured loans as permissible and their importance grew steadily. In 1935 it was accelerated by the raising of the ceiling to $100 and in the later thirties unsecured loans account for 13 to 15 percent of all personal loans outstanding.[11]

Over three fourths of the loans made by personal finance companies in 1939 were secured by chattel mortgages on household goods; if the automobile security and other chattels are

TABLE 17

WISCONSIN PERSONAL FINANCE COMPANIES' LOANS MADE, 1939, CLASSIFIED BY TYPE OF SECURITY

Type of Security	Amount of Loans Made	Percent of Total
Chattel mortgages on household goods	$9,759,792	78.6%
Automobiles	962,856	7.8
Other chattels	115,363	.9
Unsecured notes	913,739	7.4
Endorsed and/or co-maker notes	481,186	3.9
Wage assignments	16,935	.1
Other considerations	167,485	1.3
TOTAL	$12,417,359	100.0%

SOURCE: *Annual Report of Small Loan Companies* for 1939, State of Wisconsin Banking Department.

11 Their importance will probably increase as a result of the 1941 statutory revision permitting unsecured loans up to $300.

added the proportion is about 87 percent while it is only about one-fourth for credit unions (Tables 16 and 17).[12] Co-makers serve as collateral for about 4 percent of personal finance company loans while they account for about 47 percent of credit union loans outstanding. The unsecured note is only half as important a form of security for personal finance companies as for credit unions. While there are changes taking place in the security behind the loans of these cash credit agencies, the personal finance company loan still runs to chattel mortgages on personal property and the credit union loan to security by endorsers.

Repayment Experience

In order to compute the loss ratio the losses charged to the guaranty fund on personal loans were taken in a given year and compared with the volume of personal loans in the same year (Table 18). To get an accurate picture of the credit experience with a given volume of loans the ratio of losses on that particular volume should be computed. However, it is impossible to break down the data on charge-offs, so the volume of loans and charge-offs on loans in a given year are used as an approximation of the correct loss experience. Furthermore, in some years the credit unions made recoveries on accounts that were previously charged to the guaranty fund. These recoveries should be subtracted from the charge-offs in the year in which the charge-off was made, but again, it is impossible to obtain such a break-down, so consequently the recoveries have been subtracted from the charge-offs in the same year that these recoveries were made, thus obtaining a net charge-off figure.

The figure for recoveries on charge-offs is an aggregate sum and includes not only recoveries on personal loans, but also on mortgage loans and investments which were previously written

12 The data in Table 17 are broken down by volume of loans made hence are not strictly comparable with the credit union data in Table 16 which are based on loans outstanding.

off. Again a break-down on recoveries would be desirable and was not obtainable. Consultation with the Banking Department led to the conclusion that almost all the recoveries to the guaranty fund were on personal loans, hence the procedure of subtracting recoveries only from losses on personal loans introduces no significant bias in the results.

In 1938 and 1939 credit unions reported recoveries to the guaranty fund on accounts previously charged off, but for earlier years there is no information on this point. That does not mean, however, that some recoveries were not made. The credit unions lumped the recovery figures together with other figures in the undivided profit adjustment account and there was no way of segregating the recovery item; hence the charge-off figure in earlier years is overestimated by a small and insignificant amount.

From the figures available it is evident that credit union loss experience on personal loans is surprisingly small. The largest loss ratio occurred in 1939 and even in that year losses were only two-tenths of 1 percent of the total volume of personal loans. From 1929 to 1932 the loss ratio did not exceed one-hundredth of 1 percent; in 1933 and 1934 it rose to a high of seven-hundredths of 1 percent of total volume and dropped sharply thereafter. In 1938 and 1939 the loss ratio rose to about fifteen-hundredths and one-fifth of 1 percent of total volume. This latter increase in the loss ratio is the result of a change in the administrative procedures by the Banking Department. In the early thirties credit unions were under the Building and Loan Division and because this Division was not adequately equipped with personnel, the examination of credit unions' books was not stringent nor frequent. After a separate Credit Union Division was set up in the Banking Department there was stricter supervision over credit unions but still there were not enough examiners to do the job well. In the later thirties, however, more examiners were added, which meant more coverage of unions and also sounder financial practices, conse-

TABLE 18

VOLUME OF PERSONAL LOANS MADE AND LOSSES CHARGED TO GUARANTY FUND, 1929-1939

Year	Volume Personal Loans Made	Losses Charged to Guaranty Fund on Personal Loans	Percent Losses to Volume
1929	$321,616	$20.30	[a]
1930	396,196	78.04	.01
1931	476,622	59.42	.01
1932	636,455	62.73	[a]
1933	768,879	612.64	.07
1934	1,741,750	1,137.48	.06
1935	3,488,837	549.34	.01
1936	5,867,143	1,874.17	.03
1937	8,282,975	4,610.18	.05
1938	7,687,538	11,043.39[b]	.14
1939	9,811,695	22,054.57[c]	.22
TOTAL.....	$39,479,706	$42,102.26	.10

SOURCE: Files of Wisconsin State Banking Department.

[a] Less than 1/100th of 1 percent.

[b] Represents a net figure: recoveries to guaranty fund of $162 were subtracted from charges to guaranty fund in 1938.

[c] Represents a net figure: recoveries to guaranty fund of $1,732 were subtracted from charges to guaranty fund in 1939.

quently, the loss figures for 1938 and 1939 are somewhat exaggerated in an upward direction since the charge-offs resulted from the cumulation of the laxity of supervision in the earlier years. For the whole period, 1929 through 1939, the losses on the volume of personal loans made were equal to one-tenth of 1 percent.

There are certain factors related to the nature of the credit union that serve to reduce credit risks and losses. The credit committee because of its closeness to the applicant has an intimate knowledge of the more important risk elements in each individual case. Since the borrower's life is allied to all the other members of the credit union by virtue of working in the same plant, attending the same church or belonging to the same local of a labor union, by not paying his loan he is defrauding his fellow workers and thereby is inviting social ostracism which may be more painful than repaying his obligation. Many credit unions are located in the plant of the company which often takes an interest in its affairs, and therefore non-paying borrowers may more than likely come to the attention of the management than would be true if they borrowed from a small loan company or some other lending agency.

From these statistics it would appear that the credit committees of credit unions are employing an extremely conservative lending policy. If the volume of loans were increased it is conceivable that losses would not increase in proportion and net profits would rise. With a more liberalized policy the credit committees would attract increased business in two important ways: first, by adding the contribution of many potential members who are now being driven to other credit agencies; and second, by raising the fees collected from those who are already members but are not using the loan facilities of the unions because the loan requirements are too exacting.

Another reason for the low loss experience of Wisconsin credit unions is the loan protection taken out on the life of the borrower. In the event of death the credit union has been forced to collect its debt from the estate of the deceased, and since the borrower more often than not was in the low income group a burden was put on his family which was considered undesirable. Also, if there were co-signers any insistance that they make good on the loan aroused bitter feelings and created ill-will toward the credit union. On the other hand, if the credit union charged the amount off as a bad debt, the members of the credit union would be treated unjustly as their equity would be diminished.

The simplest scheme for treating this risk was to get an insurance company to insure the lives of the borrower and in that way a known cost (the price of insurance) would be substituted for the unknown risk. At first it was a difficult task to get life insurance companies to write these policies for credit unions. Credit unions were relatively unknown in the twenties, and most of them were small. In 1929 the Banker's National Life Insurance Company of New Jersey wrote policies for one Missouri credit union and in 1930 for other credit unions operating in the same state. From that year on there was a mushroom growth of this type of insurance throughout the credit union movement in the United States so that in 1935, 28 states had credit unions which were insuring the lives of their borrowers. Because of its early start the New Jersey company wrote the majority of this business.

The rate in this first policy was $1.35 per $1,000 for a loan of $1,000.[13] In the beginning, policies were written on a group basis with individual selection and the credit unions objected to the premium, claiming it was too high; their complaints were effective and the rate was subsequently reduced to $.85 per $1,000. The premium was paid by the insured member, and not by the credit union.

At the annual meeting of the Credit Union National Association in 1935 it was decided to set up an insurance company to write policies insuring the lives of credit union borrowers. On May 20, 1935, the CUNA Mutual Insurance Society, an old line[14] legal reserve mutual life insurance company was organized under Chapter 206 of the Insurance Laws of Wisconsin.

13 This meant that the average liability of the company was $500 since the loan was paid in equal monthly installments.

14 The CUNA Mutual Insurance Society is also invading the industrial life policy field. Their services are only supplied to credit union members who as individuals take out policies in amounts from $200 and over. The premium on a $200 policy for a person aged 35 would be $5.25 which is paid for life with benefits to the estate upon death. The company claims it can write these policies more cheaply than private companies since no commissions are paid, no profits paid to any individual and most of the work is done through the mails. On August 15, 1941 there were 108 policies of this type outstanding in Wisconsin and the coverage provided totalled $122,000.

The company is administered by a Board of Directors of ten elected from the members. Credit unions belonging to the State Credit Union League affiliated with the Credit Union National Association all become voting members of the insurance company; where no state leagues exist, credit unions directly affiliated with the national association are accorded the same privilege. Members of participating credit unions are offered the opportunity to purchase individual life insurance policies.

Technically the "loan protection" policy covers the credit union against loss on account of the death of the borrower up to amount of the unpaid principal of the loan outstanding plus the unpaid interest from the date of the last principal payment to the date of the origin of the claim but in no case can it exceed six months. For example, a man borrows $1,000 for ten months on January 1 and repays principal and interest for one month which leaves $900 of principal outstanding. He makes no further payments on interest or principal and dies on August 31; the insurance covers the $900 of principal and only six months interest delinquency so that the credit union receives $900 plus the interest for six months and not for August. All loans included in the credit union financial statement except those made to other than individuals are covered under the terms of the loan protection agreement. Coverage on real estate loans is optional.

The credit union as the insured executes an agreement with the CUNA Mutual Insurance Society by mail. There are no salesmen, agents, or brokers employed by the company. The Society waives rights of subrogation and does not collect losses from co-signers or other security. While there are several plans of supplying this insurance reference is made only to the two most popular.

Under the first plan the credit union pays $.75 per $1,000 per month on the total unpaid loan balances outstanding as shown in the credit union's monthly financial statement which it must submit immediately at the end of each month's business. The cost of loan protection is in almost all cases borne by the credit union as it is considered part of the operating expense so that the member makes no payment for the protection. This plan provides that death as well as total and permanent disability originating after the effective date of coverage may be accepted as a basis for claims. The total and permanent disability benefits apply to loans made to members prior to attaining age 60. Maximum coverage for one person is limited to $2,000. The second plan differs from the first in that it does not include total and permanent disability benefits. The rate is $.65 per $1,000 of loans outstanding and is computed on the basis of financial statements submitted at the end of each month by the credit union.

Most of the loan protection for credit unions in Wisconsin is written by CUNA Mutual Insurance Society which has paid 344 claims in Wisconsin amounting to $51,685 from the time of its first policy through December 31, 1940. 1936 was the first full year of operation when about 14 percent of the unions were covered by loan protection from CUNA Society; and the number increased so rapidly that by 1939 they amounted to 35 percent (Table 19). The percentage of personal loans outstanding covered by loan protection insurance with CUNA was 8.5 in 1936 and increased steadily through 1939 to account for about 40 percent of the total.

Interest Rates Paid by Borrowing Members

The Wisconsin Statute regulating credit union operations limits the interest charge on loans to a maximum rate of 1 percent per month on unpaid balances. A borrower may repay the whole or any part of his loan at any time and the law provides that when a discounted loan is repaid in full before maturity, the *pro rata* unearned portion of the interest previously deducted shall be refunded to the borrower.

The credit union can be most succinctly defined as a cooperative bank. With this interest rate limitation the credit union cannot operate like most cooperative ventures. One of the fun-

TABLE 19

INSURANCE COVERAGE OF WISCONSIN CREDIT UNIONS BY CUNA MUTUAL INSURANCE SOCIETY

Year	Number of Contracts	Percent of All Unions Covered	Amount of Coverage	Percent of Total Personal Loans Outstanding
1936	63	13.8	$269,731	8.5
1937	123	25.2	1,263,517	27.1
1938	169	31.1	1,642,361	30.2
1939	197	34.9	2,634,136	40.0

SOURCE: Files of CUNA Mutual Insurance Society.

damental principles of cooperative operations is to charge the market rate on whatever is sold and to supply a rebate to customers in the form of patronage dividend. But the going market rate or interest charge on consumer credit rendered to low income groups is somewhere between 18 and 30 percent, and if this rate were charged the main objective of the credit union would be defeated; the cost would put the service out of reach financially of the low income groups which the credit unions are trying especially to assist.

The rates actually charged by the Wisconsin credit unions are not published by the Banking Department but it was possible to obtain such information for 313 credit unions which covers about 55 percent of all organizations in 1939 (Table 20). The most common rate charged in that year was 1 percent per month on unpaid balances. About three-fourths of the unions for which such data were available charged this rate, the maximum permitted by law. The next most common rate was three-fourths of 1 percent per month on unpaid balances but only about 6 percent of all reporting organizations charged this rate and about 3.5 percent of the reporting credit unions charged .8 of 1 percent per month; 2 percent of all unions charged one-half of 1 percent per month. In addition to the 236 reporting organizations that charged a flat sum of 1 percent per month there were 31 credit unions, comprising 10 percent of all reporting organizations that charged a split rate, i. e., 1 percent on the first $125 of a loan and .5 of 1 percent on that part of the loan in excess of $125. It does not mean that a person borrowing $300 pays .5 of 1 percent while a person borrowing $100 pays 1 percent. This is not possible because the credit union is a mutual organization and everyone is given the same treatment, hence on $125 of loan all pay 1 percent; those who borrow more than $125 pay a different rate on the excess than was charged on the first $125. The utilization of the split rate has become more wide-spread with the passage of time and one reason for this has been the attempt on the part of Wisconsin credit unions to compete for the larger loans with the personal loan departments of commercial banks. Since there was no splitting of rates below $100 all loans paying a split rate must be secured and therefore could be expected to pay a lower rate than unsecured loans on which the risk is greater.

In addition to the interest paid by credit union members, some organizations employ a system of fines for delinquent accounts. Since these fines add to the cost of borrowing, they must be included in a discussion of costs of loans to members. Not all unions employ this practice but it was not possible to ascertain how many actually do. Fines amounted to .3 of 1 percent of average loans balances outstanding in 1929 and have fallen steadily so that by 1939 they were only .07 of 1 percent of average loan balances outstanding.[15]

By way of comparison it may be pointed out that there has not been any noticeable change in the interest charged on personal loans by credit unions since 1931. Of the 45 credit unions in that year for which there was information available, 40 or 88

15 See pp. 129-130 for a more detailed discussion of fines.

percent of the total were charging a rate of 1 percent per month on unpaid balances; 1 charged 1 percent a month on loans of less than $500 and .5 of 1 percent on loans of $500 or

TABLE 20

INTEREST CHARGED BY WISCONSIN CREDIT UNIONS 1939

Rate of Interest (percent per month on unpaid balances)	Number of Unions	Percent
1.0	236	75.4
1.0 on first $125 of loan; .66 on excess	1	.3
1.0 on first $100 of loan; .75 on excess	1	.3
1.0 on first $100; .75 next $100; .50 on excess	3	1.0
1.0 on first $200; .75 on excess	3	1.0
1.0 on first $300; .75 over $300 to $500; .50 on excess	3	1.0
1.0 on first $100; .75 next $400; .50 on excess	1	.3
1.0 on first $200; .75 over $200 to $300; .50 on excess	1	.3
1.0 on first $200; .75 over $200 to $300; 50 over $300	1	.3
1.0 on first $100; .75 over $100 to $300; .50 over $300	2	.6
1.0 on first $250; .50 over $250	1	.3
1.0 on first $300; .50 over $300	3	1.0
1.0 on first $500; .50 over $500	1	.3
1.0 on first $100; .4 on excess	1	.3
.90	1	.3
.87	1	.3
.85	1	.3
.83	2	.6
.80 on first $300; .5 on excess	2	.6
.80	11	3.6
.75 on first $300; .50 on excess	2	.6
.75 on first $500; .48 on excess	1	.3
.75	19	6.1
.66	3	1.0
.60	1	.3
.50	6	2.0
.33	1	.3
Graduated rate 1.0 to .50	3	1.0
Graduated rate .83 to .50	1	.3
	313	100.0

SOURCE: Files of Wisconsin State Banking Department.

over; 1 charged .75 percent per month; 2 charged .83 on loans up to $500 and .65 on sums in excess while the remaining union charged .8 of 1 percent per month. A comparison with the rates charged in 1939 shows that the lower range of rates in that year is much lower than the lower range of rates in 1931 although in both cases not many of the credit unions fell into these groups. Also in 1939 the split rate was used much more extensively to compete for the larger loans with the personal loan departments of commercial banks which had multiplied during the depression.[16]

The borrowing members in a credit union are frequently bringing pressure to lower the rates charged on personal loans. The Banking Department, the Credit Union National Association and the Wisconsin Credit Union League have advised credit unions to refrain from reducing the rate of interest charged on personal loans below 1 percent per month on unpaid balances outstanding. One of the major objections to rate reductions is that it impairs the operating efficiency of an organization. By cutting interest rates, earnings are likewise reduced and the organization may find that it cannot afford to take out borrower's life protection insurance or it cannot expend as much money as it otherwise would be able to on an educational program which is an integral part of credit unions' function in the opinion of the officials in the movement.

One of the most important reasons for maintaining interest rates on loans and thereby also net earnings is to enable the credit union to eliminate gradually the subsidy which many of them find so necessary. While a subsidy by the parent company in which the plant is located, or by some outside organization has undeniably been very helpful to many credit unions, there are too many cases where these organizations are completely

16 According to J. M. Chapman, *Commercial Banks and Consumer Financing* (New York, 1940) the personal loan department of the commercial bank is the outgrowth of the depression.

dependent on that subsidy. The organization is usually dependent upon the management to whom it looks for its continued existence and very frequently its decisions are influenced or made by the management of the plant. When the management subsidizes the organization and *if* it decides the credit union's policy by virtue of its subsidy, the members do not get much experience in the actual operation of the organization. Furthermore, it is not inconceivable that the management can, by virtue of aiding the continued existence of the credit union, make demands upon the employees such as non-unionization, etc.[17] If the credit union is important enough to the membership, they may actually submit to such demands rather than lose the services which the credit union renders to them.

While it may be necessary to acquire subsidies in the earlier stages of its life, the credit union should make a conscious effort as it progresses, to pay more and more of its own way and that will not be accomplished by reducing earnings through lowering the rates charged on loans.[18] When the credit union becomes able to pay its own way, it becomes stronger and more independent and can also undertake new ventures. If it employs part-time or full-time paid personnel, the credit union will find itself able to operate at a greater convenience to the members. If it pays rent in addition, it has a definite location, not one given out of the kindness of the plant management; it can also have fixed office hours for the members' convenience. A paid employee will probably be more adept at his function of treasurer, bookkeeper or whatever it may be, than a man who has a full-time job at which he makes his living and the credit union job where he passes his free hours as a novice. The credit union members will probably have greater faith in the paid specialist than in the novice taken from their own ranks. The

17 Such demands would, in all probability, be an unfair labor practice as defined in the National Labor Relations Act, and therefore subject to control.

18 It is also desirable to increase earnings by reducing dividends paid on investments.

members may have enough confidence in the specialist to seek his advice and guidance in credit affairs and this, if expertly given, would be of inestimable value to them. It is frequently stated that credit union members or potential members prefer to use the loan facilities extended by commercial lenders because of the financial advice also rendered by these agencies. If this is the case, then hired help that is efficient and well paid may render the credit union a proportionately greater service than the added cost. Such help can not, however, be obtained at first, by reducing interest rates.

Another objection to reducing the interest charged on loans has been that the credit union movement is harmed by the practice of one organization charging a rate of 1 percent while another union across the street or in another plant charges a lower rate. It is stated that a condition of this sort causes considerable criticism from the members of the union charging the higher rate which may, if it becomes widespread, be harmful to the credit union because of the ill-will it incites on the part of the membership.[19] It would appear that this objection to rate reductions is an attempt to penalize the efficient and low cost credit union and prevent its borrowers from reaping the benefits of this efficiency and for that reason is not tenable. It is fair, however, to object to one credit union which is no more efficient than any others from lowering its rates and thereby arousing the opposition of members of other unions. When this is done, the rate cutter is able to reduce its rate simply because it is sacrificing its possibility of becoming independent, which is inefficiency, not efficiency, and should be prevented if possible as an undesirable practice. Where, however, two credit unions are both using paid personnel, etc., and are both functioning well except that one is more efficient than the other there does not seem to be any valid objection to differential interest rates.

19 See article on interest rate policy for credit unions by E. G. Hampton in *Bulletin* of Wisconsin Credit Union League, March 28, 1939.

In 1939 two credit unions started a practice which they call "patronage dividends" which means that after dividends are paid to shareholders, an extra dividend may be paid out, not on share capital invested by members but on amounts of interest paid by borrowers. This idea originated with credit unions established in cooperatives and it is not surprising that its origins would be found in this group since the fundamental of cooperation is a return, not on the amount of money contributed to the organization but on the volume of business done with the cooperative (patronage). It is mainly a few of the larger credit unions that engage in this practice.

The Banking Department frowns upon this practice but technically a "patronage dividend" comes under the regulation of interest charged—it is a form of interest rebate. If it were a dividend, the by-laws limit dividends to 6 percent and only with special permission of the Commission can dividends in excess of this be paid; hence the practice of "patronage dividends" would be subject to Commission approval if total dividends exceeded that sum. But patronage dividends are part of the interest rate. The Commission does not appear to have any control over this practice since the credit union by-laws state that "the rate of interest charged on loans shall be determined from time to time by the board of directors."

One objection to this practice is that it reduces the earnings which might be added to the guaranty fund or undivided profit account. It would appear that retaining more of the earnings and thereby increasing the shareholders' equity in the credit union rather than disbursing these earnings immediately in cash would be a wise procedure. Further, the Banking Department has taken a firm stand against reducing interest charges, stating that it is its avowed policy to try to make credit unions more independent and self-sufficient by using their earnings to hire paid personnel and if necessary pay rent and in every possible way become independent of the management of the plant in which the union is established. It would appear that these objectives are highly desirable for the strengthening of the credit union movement. It is apparent also that becoming more self sufficient, even if not completely so, would increase the expense of operation. Under the circumstances it is easy to sympathize with the Banking Department's objection to the " patronage dividend."

To the credit unions that have sought counsel on the advisability of interest rate reductions for experimental purposes, the Banking Department has consistently pointed to the experience of the unions that have tried rate cuts before. While not all the cases have been failures, in those cases where the rate reduction did not increase borrowing, the union has found that its net earnings were adversely affected. When they attempted to restore the original interest rate, it was very difficult to accomplish because the members had become accustomed to the new rate and refused to permit it to be changed even though it meant reduced reserves and less independence.

While this experience may be a valid reason for the Banking Department's objections to experimental reductions in the cost of borrowing, it is the impression of the author that the freezing effect of a rate cut can be avoided and at the same time a reduction in interest costs to borrowers can be achieved by utilizing the " patronage dividend " method of rebating interest charges where the credit union can afford to do so without jeopardizing its financial standing. It would appear desirable, however, to revise either the credit union by-laws or Statutes to make it mandatory that the credit union obtains permission from the Banking Department before paying this patronage dividend. By incorporating this provision, the Commission will be able to prevent any abuse of patronage dividend procedure and can continue to press its claims for increasing the net earnings of credit unions to be made available for reserves or hiring of paid personnel.

CHAPTER V

MORTGAGE LOANS

WISCONSIN is one of the few states which permits credit unions to make mortgage loans against real estate; the federal credit union law does not permit such loans. Under the 1923 law, credit unions were permitted to utilize any funds not required for purpose of lending, by depositing them to the credit of the corporation in banks or trust companies incorporated under the laws of Wisconsin or in national banks located in the state or by investing these funds in securities which are legal investments for trust funds under section 231.32 of the Statutes. One of the legal investments for trust funds was real estate mortgages.

However, it was not until 1926 that credit unions made mortgage loans (Table 21). In that year the two organizations in existence, the Milwaukee Federal Employees Credit Union and the Milwaukee Municipal Credit Union, had apparently reached a saturation point in loans extended to members and preferred to invest their funds in mortgage loans rather than to hold them in cash, a non-earning asset. While the ratio of mortgage loans outstanding to total loans outstanding was only 17 percent in 1926, in the following year it jumped sharply to 75 percent of loans outstanding. While four new unions were chartered in 1927, they did not begin to operate until the closing months of the year. In 1928 the ratio of mortgage loans outstanding fell and comprised only one-fourth of all loans outstanding. Six new credit unions were added by the end of the year, making 10 in all; and since these new organizations were being called upon to use their funds to make personal loans they were not faced with cash to invest. The number of credit unions continued to rise slowly through 1931 and there was also a slow but continous rise in the ratio of mortgage loans. In 1929 about one third of all loans were mortgage loans, and by 1932 they comprised 46 percent.

TABLE 21

OUTSTANDING MORTGAGE LOANS AND ALL LOANS OF WISCONSIN CREDIT UNIONS, 1923-1939

Year Ending	Total All Loans Outstanding	Mortgage Loans Outstanding	Ratio of (2) to (1)
1923	$2,388		
1924	26,189		
1925	39,097		
1926	69,414	$12,000	17.3
1927	123,673	94,303	76.3
1928	172,495	44,900	26.0
1929	293,486	96,600	32.2
1930	416,385	186,084	40.4
1931	552,887	257,184	46.5
1932	745,696	345,097	46.3
1933	924,257	393,808	42.6
1934	1,488,108	498,666	33.5
1935	2,377,567	536,137	22.5
1936	3,663,545	524,668	14.3
1937	5,157,454	502,384	9.7
1938	5,987,760	564,732	9.4
1939	7,197,948	622,068	8.6

SOURCE: Files of Wisconsin State Banking Department.

In 1933, the statute was revised and section 186.11 was amended specifically to permit credit unions to make loans to members secured by first mortgages on real estate, with the approval of the Banking Commissioner. This amendment was apparently intended to restrict the mortgage loan business done by credit unions by limiting such loans only to members of the organization and secondly by requiring approval of the Banking Commissioner. There is some evidence that the revision of the statute accomplished its purpose. The ratio of such loans outstanding fell about 4 percent as compared with the previous year and the reason the decline is not greater is explained by the fact that the revised statute took effect June 30, 1933 hence was operative only six months.

Early in 1934 there was some dissatisfaction expressed by the banking authorities with the persistence of the practice of making mortgage loans. It was pointed out the major object of a credit union is to take care of the small loan borrowing of its members and the Commissioner directed them not to make any mortgage loans until they had satisfied the authorities that the small loan needs of members were taken care of. It was stated further that this type of investment ties up funds for a long period of time and cannot ordinarily be liquidated upon short enough notice in the event there is a substantial withdrawal of shares by the members.

The ratio of mortgage loans outstanding fell further in 1934 and accounted for one-third of all loans outstanding, declined to less than one-fourth of all loans outstanding in 1935 and to about 15 percent in 1936. The Commissioner apparently felt that his recommendations of 1934 were not yielding the results desired and on December 4, 1936 the Banking Commission promulgated a set of rules and regulations prescribing the conduct of business of credit unions operating under Chapter 186 Revised Statutes of Wisconsin.[1] The Commission interpreted the intent and purpose of Chapter 186 Revised Statutes, as being " primarily to not only promote thrift among the members of credit unions, but more particularly to furnish consumer credit for necessitous purposes to such members." It was further stated that certain credit unions were making real estate mortgage loans, in some cases without the permission and consent of the Commission and often in amounts which impoverished the funds of these organizations for the purpose of making small loans for " necessitous " purposes.

The Commission's order, which intended to restrict the mortgage lending by credit unions stated that:

1 These rules and regulations were issued by the Commission after a study of mortgage loans was not only made by it but also by a Committee appointed from the Credit Union State League and the Credit Union Advisory Committee.

1. No credit union with assets of $25,000 or under shall make any investments in real estate mortgages to members except and only as authorized and approved by the Banking Commission.
2. Credit unions with assets in excess of $25,000 may invest in real estate mortgages to members out of surplus funds but in no case shall the total aggregate real estate loans of the organization exceed 20 percent of the total assets of that credit union. The maximum size of such real estate mortgage loans shall be $2,000 and the maximum maturity shall be 24 months; the Banking Commission must approve all renewals of mortgages.
3. Any credit union whose total aggregate investment in real estate mortgage loans exceeds the limitations found in paragraphs (1) and (2) above shall proceed to liquidate such mortgages in an orderly manner "consistent with good business methods" and shall refrain from investing in any new real estate mortgages until the total aggregate of such investments conforms to the provisions set forth above.
4. Except as permitted by this order or upon express approval of the Commission, every credit union shall keep its funds liquid and shall invest them in small loans to members for "necessitous" purposes.

These restrictions were roundly condemned by the larger and older organizations who had long since found this field a convenient and lucrative outlet for their idle funds. The most voluble critics were the credit unions located in Milwaukee where in 1939, 13 of the 34 credit unions making mortgage loans accounted for 88 percent of all mortgage loans outstanding in that year.

In order to meet the objections of these organizations, the Commission issued a new order, effective September 2, 1937 which relaxed the restrictions on real estate mortgage investments to a degree. The maximum size of loans was raised to

$3,000 and the maturity increased to 36 months. The requirement that credit unions liquidate real estate mortgage loans in excess of the sums specified in the 1936 order was also modified to permit new mortgage loans providing that the aggregate amount of total mortgages outstanding compared with the assets of the credit union would be reduced at least 10 percent each year.

The larger unions were still not satisfied and in August, 1939 they were again successful in having the restrictions on real estate loans relaxed. A new order was issued by the Commission allowing real estate loans up to 25 percent of the total assets of each union with assets over $25,000 and the maturity was extended to 5 years provided that the loans were amortized at a monthly rate sufficient to equal at least 50 percent over the period. Despite this amendment, the ratio of mortgage loans outstanding continued to fall, reaching a new low of 9 percent at the end of 1939.[2]

2 In April 1941, the Commission repealed all previously adopted rules and regulations and drew up a completely new set to supplement Section 186.11 of Chapter 186, Revised Statutes of Wisconsin, for 1935. They represent further concessions to the larger and older credit unions which have continuously fought for greater outlets for investments in the real estate mortgage loan business. The new provisions state that:

1. Credit unions with assets under $25,000 shall not make real estate mortgage loans.
2. Loan extension practice is specifically outlined. The following instruments must be obtained on each mortgage loan by any credit union:
   - A. An attorney's opinion indicating that the union has a first and paramount lien.
   - B. Abstract of title or title guaranty policy which must indicate the credit union mortgage loan.
   - C. The mortgage instrument properly signed and recorded.
   - D. The bond or note properly signed.
   - E. Sufficient fire and wind storm insurance to adequately protect the credit union loan. These insurance policies must contain a loss payable clause in favor of the credit union.
   - F. Adequate evidence must be on file to prove that the current taxes have been paid and in addition, a tax record must be maintained to indicate thereafter the tax payment record.

While the absolute amount of mortgage loans outstanding increased steadily total loans outstanding increased more rapidly due to the fact that many new unions were being formed during the period and the new credit union members wanted personal loans, with the result that the proportion of mortgage loans to all loans outstanding declined.

Mortgage Loan Practice

In surveying mortgage loans against real estate it was possible to obtain information for 33 of the 34 unions having such loans outstanding at the end of 1939. Most of the loans extended against real estate were first mortgages. Twenty-nine institutions extended only first mortgage loans while the remaining four also made second mortgage loans. Twenty-six unions required the property against which loans had been made to be covered by fire and cyclone insurance. Two institutions made exceptions in certain cases while a third union had extended a real estate loan against unimproved property hence did not re-

---

G. A signed appraisal of the property must be included in each mortgage loan packet.

3. Care must be exercised to comply with all sound mortgage lending practices.
   A. All property in Milwaukee County on which real estate loans are made must be appraised by appraisors recommended by or approved of by the Banking Commission; in other counties two competent appraisors, not members of the credit union, can be employed. Appraisals shall separate the land and improvements and shall state the estimated current market value.
   B. Maximum mortgage loan shall be two-thirds of appraised value.
   C. No mortgage loans shall be made on real estate located more than 25 miles from lending organization's office.
4. Organizations with assets of from $25,000 to $120,000 may make mortgage loans to members out of surplus funds only in amounts up to $3,000 per member; credit unions with assets in excess of $120,000 may not make a loan which exceeds in size 2½ percent of total assets and in no case above $5,000. No more than one loan may be made to any one member and the loans must be amortized by regular monthly payments at least equal to $10 per month per $1,000 of the original principal amount.

quire such insurance. Four unions did not demand their real estate borrowers to have their property insured. Twenty-nine required the prospective borrowers to furnish an abstract of title to the property, 1 made a few exceptions to this general rule and 3 did not require such a document.

While there is some variation displayed by the 33 mortgage lending credit unions in the percentage of valuation of property against which real estate loans are limited, 9 credit unions set the maximum at 60 percent and another 9 at 50 percent. Two unions reported no maximum amount set, 1 permitted loans up to 100 percent of valuation, 4 permitted loans up to 70 percent while 1 set the figure at 25 percent. Of the remaining 7 institutions the maximum percent of valuation varied from 55 to 90 percent.

These same unions reported the method of appraising the property against which real estate loans were to be made. In 13 unions the credit committee of the organization served as the appraising body; 7 used the board of directors and in 2 cases the appraisal committee was composed of the directors and the credit committee. Five unions established a separate appraisal committee drawn from the membership of the union while 4 institutions simply used the assessment roll established by the city for tax collection purposes.

It was possible to get a break-down of the size of mortgage loan made for 24 credit unions. This information is presented in Table 22 and it refers to the size of loan when it was originally made; in many cases, therefore, these loans were made in years prior to 1939. About one-third of the loans were $1,500 or under, while about one-half the loans were in excess of $2,500. Slightly more than one-fourth of these loans were for between $1,501 and $2,500.

By tracing the credit union reports back to earlier periods it was possible to get a break-down for 16 credit unions of the maturity of the mortgage loans at the time they were made. Approximately four-fifths of the loans of these unions had a

TABLE 22

NUMBER OF MORTGAGE LOANS OUTSTANDING, DECEMBER 31, 1939
CLASSIFIED BY SIZE AT TIME MADE

Size in dollars	Percent of total
$1 — 500	5.5
501 — 1,000	13.6
1,001 — 1,500	13.6
1,501 — 2,000	14.7
2,001 — 2,500	13.2
2,501 — 3,000	18.4
Over 3,000	21.0
TOTAL	100.0

SOURCE: Files of Wisconsin State Banking Department.

maturity of 30 months or more while the remainder had maturities ranging from over 6 months to 24 months.

TABLE 23

NUMBER OF MORTGAGE LOANS OUTSTANDING, DECEMBER 31, 1939
CLASSIFIED BY MATURITY AT TIME MADE

Number of Months	Percent of Total
1 — 6	..
Over 6 — 12	.9
Over 12 — 18	3.7
Over 18 — 24	14.7
Over 24 — 30	..
Over 30 — 36	50.4
Over 36	30.3
TOTAL	100.0

SOURCE: Files of Wisconsin State Banking Department.

RATES OF CHARGE

Nine-tenths of all credit unions making mortgage loans against real estate charged 6 percent per annum or less interest. One organization charged 10 percent and another charged 12 percent. The modal charge was 6 percent and around three-fifths of all institutions made loans at that rate. One-fifth of the unions made loans at 5 percent.

There was a noticeable reduction in the rate of interest on mortgage loans during the thirties. Of the ten credit unions for which information was available in 1931, three charged 12 percent per annum, one 8 percent, three charged 7.2 percent while the remaining three charged 6 percent per annum. The reduction in rates charged was due to the competition of other mortgage lending institutions, including governmental agencies and also the general decline in interest rates during the depression.

In comparing the rates by the same credit unions, one would expect the charges on real estate loans to be lower than on personal loans since rates on real estate loans are usually lower in the commercial money market. One union charged 12 percent per annum and another 10 percent on both personal and real estate loans. It is difficult to understand how customers could be obtained at these rates except insofar as the market for this type of credit is imperfectly competitive, or the credit unions were taking the poorer credit risks hence charged higher rates on these loans.

TABLE 24

RATES OF CHARGE ON MORTGAGE LOANS OUTSTANDING DECEMBER 31, 1939

Interest Rate Per Annum	Number of Unions	Percent of Total
4½ to 6%	1	3.0
4.8%	1	3.0
5.0%	6	18.3
5.0 to 6%	1	3.0
5.4%	1	3.0
5½%	1	3.0
6%	20	60.7
10%	1	3.0
12%	1	3.0
	33	100.0

SOURCE: Files of Wisconsin State Banking Department.

Of the 20 credit unions charging 6 percent per annum on real estate loans 11 charged 12 percent per annum on personal loans, 1 charged 9.6 percent, 4 charged 9.0 percent while the other 4 charged graduated rates which ranged from 6 to 12 percent per annum depending upon the size of the personal loan. Of the 6 organizations charging 5 percent on mortgage loans, 2 charged 12 percent on personal loans, 1 charged 10 percent, 1 charged 6 percent while the other 2 had graduated charges depending upon the size of the loan but the rate on personal loans was never below that on mortgage loans. For the remaining unions it was similarly true that charges on personal loans exceeded the rates charged on mortgage loans.

Characteristics of Credit Unions Making Mortgage Loans

There was a marked geographic concentration of credit unions extending loans against real estate mortgages. At the end of 1939 there were 34 organizations with mortgage loans outstanding equal to $622,068. Thirteen of these organizations accounting for 88 percent of the total outstandings were located in Milwaukee. Only 1 credit union having mortgage loans outstanding in 1939 was located in a town with a population under 10,000. Thus it appears that their activity was concentrated on urban real estate financing.

Another noticeable feature of Wisconsin credit unions with mortgage loans outstanding in 1939 is that they were mainly older unions. While two-fifths of all organizations at the end of 1939 were under 4 years of age, only 3 percent of the unions with mortgage loans were in this age group; less than 2 percent of all unions were in existence 10 years or more, and about 20 percent of those making mortgage loans were in this category. Seventy percent of the unions formed in 1929 or earlier showed mortgage loans in their balance sheets. Apparently as the credit unions grow older their resources continue to expand since they pay fairly high dividends but they reach a saturation point as regards loans to members and therefore find it necessary to invest in some earning asset. The older the credit union, other things being equal, the larger will be the guaranty fund set aside from annual earnings. The fund can be kept in cash or invested in specified securities or real estate mortgage loans. Since cash is not an earning asset, and securities were selling at low yields, part of the guaranty fund was invested in real estate loans.

Mortgage loans are made only by the larger credit unions. Thirty percent of all credit unions at the end of 1939 had assets under $2,500 yet none of the 34 organizations having mortgage loans outstanding fell into that size category. Exactly one-half of the 34 unions had assets of $50,000 or more while only 6 percent of all unions were in this group. The size of organizations making real estate loans can be explained by reference to the surplus of funds in excess of the loan needs of the members of the larger unions and also the statutes prevent any of the smaller unions from making such loans since no credit union with assets under $25,000 is permitted by order of the Banking Department to make real estate mortgage loans.[3]

A frequency distribution of potential membership in these 34 organizations was made and it was cross classified by the ratio of actual to potential members. The most outstanding feature of credit unions having mortgage loans is the large potential membership in such organizations. While only 20 percent of all unions had a potential membership over 700, 65 percent of the organizations extending mortgage loans fell into the group.

More important than the number of potential members is the number of actual members in the organization. For all credit unions in Wisconsin the ratio of actual to potential membership

3 There were 6 credit unions in 1939 with assets of less than $25,000 which had mortgage loans outstanding. Four of them had made these loans before the 1933 law went into effect and were permitted under previously existing statutes. The remaining had, however, made their loans after 1933 and in each instance were given specific permission by the Commission.

declined as the potential membership increased. This pattern was not followed for the 34 credit unions which made mortgage loans. In no case did the ratio of actual to potential membership fall below 41 percent which appears to be conclusive evidence that these organizations are stimulating the interest of a substantial proportion of their potential members. About 30 percent of these organizations were getting 40 to 60 percent of potential members, around 25 percent had 61 to 80 percent of potential members while fully 45 percent got from 81 to 100 percent of potential members to join. In view of the reciprocal relationship between potential membership and the ratio of actual to potential membership for all credit unions, the experience of the 34 mortgage lending organizations is quite outstanding.

All credit unions in 1939 having over 400 members comprised about 13 percent of the total while about 40 percent of the 34 unions having mortgage loans had 400 or more mem-

TABLE 25

WISCONSIN CREDIT UNIONS HAVING MORTGAGE LOANS OUTSTANDING ON DECEMBER 31, 1939, CLASSIFIED BY POTENTIAL MEMBERSHIP AND RATIO OF ACTUAL TO POTENTIAL MEMBERS

Potential Members	Number of Unions	Percent	Ratio of Actual to Potential Members				
			1-20	21-40	41-60	61-80	81-100
1—100	5	14.7			1	2	2
101—200	3	8.8				1	2
201—300							
301—400	3	8.8				1	2
401—500							
501—600							
601—700	1	2.9					1
Over 700	22	64.8			9	5	8
TOTAL	34	100.0					

SOURCE: Files of Wisconsin State Banking Department.

bers. As was true for potential membership, the credit unions making mortgage loans were definitely the larger ones judged by number of members. With respect to the number of members that were borrowers there was a smaller proportion of cases fitting into the categories 1 to 15 percent and 16 to 30 for the 34 unions than for all unions. It is apparent then that the borrowing members were greater for the mortgage lending unions than for all unions in the category up to 30 percent. There were proportionately fewer cases of a borrower to member ratio over 75 percent for the 34 unions than for all unions. This fact is not surprising because if all members borrowed there would not be any surplus funds available for investment in mortgage loans. The heaviest concentration of borrowers to members for all unions and the mortgage lending institutions is found in the 31 to 45 and 46 to 60 ratio, with all unions having a higher frequency of borrowing members in the 61 to 75 percent category.

Therefore it appears that mortgage lending credit unions not only have the greatest number of potential members but also of actual members with a heavy concentration of borrowers in the 31 to 60 percent of members group. What has happened in these unions is that people have joined as a means of investing their savings at a fairly high return with many members not using the loan facilities at all. When this happens we find the credit union has become a thrift institution and is not stressing the second function for which it is organized, namely to lend sums of money for necessitous purposes.

That the credit unions making mortgage loans have surplus funds is evidenced by the fact that in 1939, 18 of the 34 unions making such loans also made investments in securities. Despite the mortgage loans and investments made, 13 of the 18 unions had more than 5 percent of their assets in cash. Of the 16 unions making mortgage loans but not making investments in securities 10 had more than 5 percent of their assets in cash.

TABLE 26

WISCONSIN CREDIT UNIONS HAVING MORTGAGE LOANS OUTSTANDING ON DECEMBER 31, 1939, CLASSIFIED BY ACTUAL MEMBERSHIP AND RATIO OF BORROWERS TO MEMBERS

Actual Members	Number of Unions	Percent	Ratio of Borrowers to Members					
			1-15	16-30	31-45	46-60	61-75	Over 75
0— 49	4	11.8			2	2		
50— 99	5	14.8			2		2	1
100—149	2	5.8			1		1	
150—199	2	5.8				2		
200—249	2	5.8			1		1	
250—299	1	2.9			1			
300—349	1	2.9				1		
350—399	3	8.8				2	1	
400 and over	14	41.3		1	7	4	2	
TOTAL	34	100.0						

SOURCE: Files of Wisconsin State Banking Department.

LOAN EXPERIENCE

In assessing the experience of credit unions extending mortgage loans the amount of losses on these loans charged to the guaranty fund were contrasted with the volume of mortgage loans made in the year the charge-off was reported. In order to get a correct picture of charge-offs in relation to mortgage loans, the charge-offs should be compared with the volume of loans made in the year that the loan which was charged off, was made. It is impossible to obtain such data, hence the figure on losses in a given year is compared with the volume of mortgage loans made in that year, since this gives an idea of loss experience on mortgage loans although it does not relate these losses to the specific loans made. Losses on mortgage loans are not charged to the guaranty fund until the property is foreclosed and disposed of. There is always a very lengthy period elapsing before the actual loss is charged off since in Wisconsin it takes at least 18 months to get title to the property, and more time elapses before a buyer is obtained. When the property is finally sold, the loss is put on the books of the credit union.

Despite the fact that Wisconsin credit unions had been making mortgage loans against real estate since 1926, the first year in which a loss was incurred was 1935 (Table 27). One reason no losses were charged to the guaranty fund on mortgage loans before 1935 is that most of such loans in the early period were made to federal government employees, and their incomes were not adversely affected by the depression, and the loans were repaid.

Beginning with 1935, however, losses on mortgage loans were charged to the guaranty fund in every year. The losses were not very large and the relatively large ones were concen-

TABLE 27

LOSSES CHARGED TO GUARANTY FUND ON MORTGAGE LOANS MADE FROM 1929 THROUGH 1939

Year	Volume of Mortgage Loans Made	Losses Charged to Guaranty Fund on Mortgage Loans	Percentage Losses to Loans Made
1929	$55,600		
1930	81,494		
1931	124,696		
1932	117,689		
1933	100,883		
1934	180,312		
1935	134,990	$693	.51
1936	79,139	521	.65
1937	84,838	852	1.00
1938	203,055	142	.06
1939	187,256	81	.04
TOTAL	$1,349,952	$2,289	.16

SOURCE: Files of the Wisconsin State Banking Department.

trated in 1935, 1936 and 1937. At the very height, in 1937, the losses were equal to 1 percent of the total volume of mortgage loans made. Thereafter they fell to insignificant amounts.

While the losses cover all mortgage loans made by Wisconsin credit unions since 1923, Table 27 merely presents the volume of such loans made since 1929; hence using this figure on volume as a denominator while the numerator includes losses on all mortgage loans, distorts the percent of losses by making it appear larger than it would be if the 1923-39 mortgage loan volume figure were used. Despite this bias the losses were only 16/100 of 1 percent of the total volume of loans made.

CHAPTER VI

INVESTMENTS

INVESTMENTS in securities, like mortgage loans on real estate, are not considered an integral part of the credit union business. It is almost universally agreed, however, that credit unions may make investments in securities, while this unanimity of opinion is not the case with regard to mortgage loans. The reason for permitting investments in securities is to enable credit unions which have funds in excess of members' demand for loans to have an outlet for profitable investment of these funds rather than to hold cash, a non-earning asset.

Since the Statutes and the Banking Commission's orders regulate the investment practices of credit unions, it is necessary to review briefly the changes in them that are relevant to the problem. From 1923 to 1933 the Statutes permitted credit unions to utilize any funds not required for loan purposes in the following manner:

(a) deposited in any bank or trust company chartered by the State of Wisconsin or in any national bank operating within the state.

(b) invested in securities which are legal investments for trust funds.

In line with provision (b) above, credit unions were empowered to invest in the following securities:

1. Federal obligations as well as the obligations of any state governments except Nevada and Wyoming.
2. Direct obligations of any political subdivisions of the State of Wisconsin.
3. Stock of any Wisconsin Building and Loan Association.
4. Bonds of Federal or joint stock land banks.
5. Mortgage bonds of railroads with more than 500 miles of track which paid dividends upon entire capital stock for 10 years preceding investment.

6. Mortgage bonds of specified public utility or street railway corporations.
7. Obligations secured by first real estate mortgages.
8. Promissory notes amply secured by the pledge of any of the bonds, real estate mortgages or securities in which investment is authorized.

In Table 28 data are presented showing the investments outstanding of Wisconsin credit unions from 1929 through 1939, classified by type. In 1931 over 60 percent of the total investments outstanding consisted of other securities; by 1932 the ratio had risen to approximately three-fourths and remained around this figure at the end of 1933. In 1931, the other securities consisted of demand or time notes of the parent company in which the union was located, corporation bonds and real estate mortgage bonds. In 1932 the major portion of the other securities portfolios consisted of real estate mortgage bonds while most of the remainder was taken up by corporation bonds. The same distribution was true for 1933.

Since the Constitution of Wisconsin forbids the issuance of bonds by the state, we find that the Wisconsin credit unions can only invest in the obligations of the political subdivisions of the state which do issue securities. In 1931 over one-third of the investments outstanding consisted of bonds issued by the municipalities of the state; by 1932 the figure fell to less than one-fourth and by 1933 to less than one-fifth. The yield on corporate bonds was higher than on municipal bonds,[1] which explains the larger proportion of other securities held by credit unions during this period. In addition, the substantial portion of municipal obligations held is accounted for by a relatively few large institutions which were extremely conservative in their investment practices. These few but large organizations were not primarily interested in yields but were more concerned

1 Municipal securities were in great demand since the income derived from them was exempt from the federal income tax.

TABLE 28

WISCONSIN CREDIT UNION INVESTMENTS OUTSTANDING, 1929-1939, CLASSIFIED BY TYPE

Year	Total Investments Outstanding	Type of Security: U.S. Govt. (Percent of Total)	Munic-ipal	Other Securities	Total
1929	$28,619				
1930	45,592				
1931	88,996	1.1	36.8	62.1	100.0%
1932	89,697	2.1	24.4	73.5	100.0
1933	91,243	6.2	19.7	74.1	100.0
1934	118,428	17.9	40.0	42.1	100.0
1935	132,970	33.0	33.4	35.6	100.0
1936	230,833	58.8	13.8	27.4	100.0
1937	408,173	61.0	7.0	32.0	100.0
1938	480,393	56.9	7.2	35.9	100.0
1939	694,302	55.5	6.4	38.1	100.0

SOURCE: Files of the Wisconsin State Banking Department.

about capital fluctuations and had sufficient investments in municipals to influence the percentage of total investments consisting of municipal securities.

Investments in federal government obligations which made up only 1 percent of total investments in 1931, rose slightly through 1933 and accounted for about 6 percent of investments at the end of that year. The low yields on governments during this period served to discourage unions from investing their funds in these obligations, coupled with the fact that the credit unions did not at that time realize the importance of liquidity in investment policy.

In 1933 several credit unions experienced difficulties with their investment accounts and the Commission became somewhat concerned lest the former trend of investments be continued in the future. It was felt that many unions might find themselves in difficult financial straits because of the heavy depreciation on the investments in other securities. The Wisconsin credit union Statute relating to investments was revised in 1933 and these organizations were limited to investments in United States government securities, municipal bonds issued by municipalities of Wisconsin and such other securities as were approved by the Commission. While the Statute did not intend to prevent credit unions from investing in securities other than government and municipal bonds, it was desired to have the authorities supervise the acquisition of such securities by credit unions.

For a short period after the 1933 revision of the Statute, the Banking Commission permitted credit unions to invest in the common and preferred stock of the company in which the credit union was operating. For the corporation this procedure served as a means of indirectly getting employees to participate in the company as vicarious owners. It thus served a purpose similar to employees stock holding and was considered as a useful phase of amicable industrial relations between employer and employee. The error of permitting such an investment policy was brought to the attention of the Banking Department by the unfortunate experience of a number of credit unions with the capital depreciation of the shares of their parent company. This experience was also unfortunate for the companies because they incurred the ill will of employee credit union members who resented the depreciation of the assets behind their shareholdings. As a result the Banking Department changed its policy with respect to investments in " such other securities as approved by the commissioner " found in the 1933 statute. Investments were permitted only in corporate bonds that were rated Grade A, or AA, or AAA in any standard bond rating book and whose record for the ten years prior to investment was such as to indicate continued ability to meet payments as they would come due.

In 1936 some credit unions were using their resources to purchase bonds. While they were formed primarily to lend money to members for "necessitous" purposes, they practically eliminated their personal loan accounts. The problem had become so acute that these organizations, mainly the smaller ones, were reminded in a Banking Commission order, dated December 4, 1936, that they were not to buy other securities until the Commission had granted them a permit.[2]

Beginning with 1934 there were marked changes in the distribution of types of securities which comprised the investment portfolio of credit unions. The restrictions imposed upon their investments in the 1933 Statute and in the subsequent Commission rulings led to a very sharp decline in investments in other securities. By 1934, this account fell by about 30 percent as compared with 1933 and comprised only about two-fifths of total investments outstanding. The "other security" account continued to decline and reached a low of about one-fourth of all investments at the end of 1936 and then steadily increased until they comprised 38 percent of investments in 1939. Throughout the later thirties newly acquired other securities consisted mainly of grade A, AA, or AAA corporate bonds.

When the Banking Department instituted its restrictions on investment in other securities, by credit unions, the organizations desiring to continue investments placed their funds in the obligations of Wisconsin municipalities and the federal government. In 1934 investments in municipal obligations accounted for two-fifths of the total in that year but thereafter the proportion declined, falling about 7 percent in 1935, 20 percent in 1936 and about 7 percent in 1937; by 1939 these obligations accounted for only 6 percent of all investments outstanding. The explanation of the very marked decline in the municipal obligation account lies in the very low yield on these bonds.

2 The Banking Department was subjected to much wrangling and disagreement with the credit unions as to what constituted a Grade A, AA, AAA bond so that a new policy regarding investments in other securities was instituted in 1940. Since that time credit union investments are limited to United States government and Wisconsin municipal obligations and within certain limits, shares of any savings and loan association.

In 1934 credit union investments in obligations of the federal government increased by about 12 percent and were equal to about 18 percent of all investments. The proportion of such holdings continued to rise steadily so that by the end of 1937 they accounted for over 60 percent of all investments. One of the popular securities held by credit unions, during this rise, was the savings bond.[3] The great increase in the proportion of federal government securities held can be accounted for by several factors. First, there were restrictions placed upon the purchase of other securities. Second, the large premiums on municipal obligations made their yields much less attractive than those of federal securities. Third, the large scale deficit financing of the federal government supplied credit unions as well as all other investors with a large quantity of its obligations which were readily available. Finally, credit unions, by virtue of their longer experience had become more sophisticated investors and had come to appreciate that the criteria of a wise investment policy stressed the importance of liquidity as well as yield.

Characteristics of Credit Unions Making Investments

As was pointed out in discussing the characteristics of credit unions making real estate mortgage loans, there is also a heavy geographic concentration of unions making investments in securities. At the end of 1939 there were 66 organizations having investments in securities outstanding; 36 of them, about 55 percent of the total, were located in Milwaukee. They accounted for 77 percent of total investments in securities outstanding.

Credit unions having investments in securities outstanding at the end of 1939 were usually the older organizations. On the average, however, they were not as old as unions showing mortgage loans. Two-fifths of all credit unions at the end of 1939 were under 4 years of age but only about eight percent of unions showing investments fell into this group while only three per-

3 Because of a Treasury ruling in May, 1940, credit unions can no longer purchase savings bonds but can acquire United States defense bonds.

cent of the mortgage lending unions were found in this category. Less than two percent of all unions were 10 or more years old while eight percent of the organizations making investments and one-fifth of all mortgage lending unions fell into this age group. Less than three-fifths of all unions were from 4 to less than 8 years old but four-fifths of all investment making unions and three-fourths of all mortgage lending unions were grouped in that category.

There are several reasons that serve to explain the relatively younger age of investment holding credit unions as contrasted with mortgage lending institutions. The younger organizations which have funds in excess of the members' demands for loans are usually reluctant to undertake mortgage lending because of the greater degree of investment acumen required in extending this type of loan. Also mortgage loans usually tie up their funds for longer periods of time than is true for prime securities which are ordinarily marketable upon short notice. Since the Commission ruling prevents credit unions with less than $25,000 of assets from making mortgage loans, the younger unions, which generally speaking are smaller than older organizations, cannot make mortgage loans against real estate even though they have surplus funds because their total assets are in many cases not in excess of the minimum required. When this happens such credit unions are forced to hold the nonearning asset, cash, or invest in securities, which is usually preferrable to complete liquidity.

Credit unions having investments outstanding at the end of 1939 were larger, on the average, than all credit unions but were smaller than those organizations making loans against real estate mortgages. Fifteen percent of all credit unions had assets of under $1,000 while there were no investment holding institutions in this size group. About seventy percent of all unions had assets of $1,000 to $24,999; forty-six percent of investment making unions fitted into this group while less than twenty percent of the unions making mortgage loans were found in this size group. One of the reasons why there were fewer unions of this size group making mortgage loans than making investments is the Commission prohibition against making loans since 1933 by unions having under $25,000 in assets. Twenty-one percent of the unions making investments had assets of $100,000 or over while thirty-two percent of the mortgage lending organizations and only three percent of all unions fell into this size category.

Further evidence that the 66 credit unions having investments in securities outstanding are organizations with surplus funds lies in the fact that 18 of them also made mortgage loans against real estate. Around seventy percent of the remaining 48 organizations had more than ten percent of their assets in cash. Apparently many of those institutions could not or would not make mortgage loans although their investments in securities did not absorb all of their idle funds.

In order to determine whether there were any unusual features relating to those 66 unions having investments in securities at the end of 1939, resort was had to the procedure employed in analyzing the same factors in the case of mortgage lending credit unions. One feature of the 66 credit unions was their relatively large potential membership. While only about twenty percent of all unions had a potential membership of 700 or more, fifty-one percent of the investment holding institutions fell into this group. This figure is somewhat smaller than that for the credit unions making mortgage loans against real estate.

For all credit unions the ratio of actual to potential membership decreases as the absolute number of potential members increases. With respect to the 66 unions examined this is not so clearly the case. It is only for credit unions having a potential membership of 700 or more that the ratio of actual to potential members falls to one to twenty percent. In about forty percent of the 66 unions a ratio of 81 to 100 is attained. About one-fifth of the unions were getting 61 to 80 percent of potential members to join while slightly under thirty percent were getting 41 to 60 percent of their potential membership to join. It is evident that investment making credit unions not only had a large potential membership but were also stimulating the interest of substantial proportions of their potential membership to join. However, the potential membership figures and the ratio of actual to potential members was not as large as for mortgage lending organizations.

TABLE 29

WISCONSIN CREDIT UNIONS HAVING INVESTMENTS OUTSTANDING ON DECEMBER 31, 1939 CLASSIFIED BY ACTUAL MEMBERSHIP AND RATIO OF BORROWERS TO MEMBERS

Actual	Number of		Ratio of Borrowers to Members					
Members	Unions	Percent	1-15	16-30	31-45	46-60	61-75	Over 75
0— 49	9	13.6		3	2	2	2	
50— 99	14	21.2		1	8	3	1	1
100—149	5	7.6			1	3	1	
150—199	8	12.2			3	5		
200—249	5	7.5		2		3		
250—299	2	3.1			2			
300—349								
350—399	3	4.5				2	1	
400 and over	20	30.3		3	8	8	1	
TOTAL	66	100.0						

SOURCE: Files of the Wisconsin State Banking Department.

About thirty percent of the 66 investment making credit unions had an actual membership of 400 or over. This figure is much higher than for all credit unions which had only thirteen percent of the total comprising this group but somewhat smaller than the 34 unions showing mortgage loans outstanding. The 66 institutions do not show any marked differences from all credit unions with respect to the number of members actually borrowing money. Since the actual number of members is higher, the investment making institutions have more surplus funds on hand which are invested in earning assets.

TABLE 30

WISCONSIN CREDIT UNIONS HAVING INVESTMENTS OUTSTANDING ON DECEMBER 31, 1939, CLASSIFIED BY POTENTIAL MEMBERSHIP AND RATIO OF ACTUAL TO POTENTIAL MEMBERS

Potential Members	Number of Unions	Percent	Ratio of Actual to Potential Members 1-20	21-40	41-60	61-80	81-100
1—100	8	12.0			1	1	6
101—200	5	8.2					5
201—300	8	12.0			2	3	3
301—400	2	3.0		1			1
401—500	3	4.5		2		1	
501—600	4	6.0			1	3	
601—700	2	3.0				1	1
Over 700	34	51.3	2	3	13	5	11
TOTAL	66	100.0					

SOURCE: Files of Wisconsin State Banking Department.

INVESTMENT EXPERIENCE

In order to assess the investment experience of Wisconsin credit unions, data were obtained on the amount of losses on investments that was charged to the guaranty fund. Such losses would arise from three types of cases. When the Banking Department examines a credit union, the examiner has a schedule which lists the par, book, and market value of the securities held by that organization. The book value is ordinarily the original cost of the security.[4] If the market value of the security is be-

4 There are a few exceptions to this generalization. The credit union may purchase a security at a premium and enter the security on its books at par and then establish a premium account for the difference between par value and actual cost. This premium is then amortized from annual earnings. A second method employed for handling the same problem is to enter the security at original cost and amortize the book value from annual earnings until it is decreased to par.

low the book value the credit union is ordered to do one of two things: to charge off to the guaranty fund the difference between book and market value, or to set up a valuation reserve equal to the difference between book and market value. This reserve is established by charges against net earnings and when this procedure is followed losses on investments are not charged against the guaranty fund. Since both procedures are used in revaluing security investments, the only way to get a correct picture of actual investment losses would be to ascertain the monetary value of losses which are treated by setting up a valuation reserve and add that figure to losses on investments actually charged to the guaranty fund. However it is not possible to obtain these data, hence the reported figure on losses on investments is used and the reader must be cautioned that the loss figure therefore represents an understatement.

The second way in which losses charged to the guaranty fund would be incurred is when the Banking Department orders a credit union, which is holding what the Commission considers undesirable securities, for whatever reason, to sell them and the sale is consummated at a price below original purchase price or current valuation on the union's book. Finally, a few losses have arisen in cases where the credit union bought securities containing a call privilege and the securities were called by the issuer at a price below the purchase price thereby creating a deficit which was charged to the guaranty fund.

The total amount of loss on investment charged to the guaranty fund is very small, amounting to only $5,614 from 1929 through 1939 (Table 31). Incidentally the period covered is one in which there was a marked deflation in security values and we would expect the figures to be much higher. This is particularly true in view of the general lack of banking and financial knowledge that characterizes the rank and file of credit union officers and managers.

In order to get a more accurate picture of actual losses on investments, irrespective of whether or not they are charged to the guaranty fund, an estimate was made of those losses which are accounted for by setting up a valuation reserve. The losses charged to the guaranty fund resulted from three types of cases, but the most important one was where the credit union marked investments down to current market values. From discussions with the authorities in the Banking Department, it is calculated that losses treated by setting up valuation reserves are about equal to losses actually charged to the guaranty fund in revaluing current investments. By being ultra conservative, even if it is assumed that losses cared for by setting up a reserve were equal to losses actually charged to the guaranty fund, the total actual loss on investments would not exceed $11,200.

TABLE 31

LOSSES ON INVESTMENTS TO TOTAL INVESTMENTS OUTSTANDING FOR WISCONSIN CREDIT UNIONS FROM 1929 THROUGH 1939

Year	Total Investments Outstanding	Losses on Investments Charged to Guaranty Fund	Ratio of Losses to Outstandings
1929	$28,619	$66.80	.23
1930	45,592	35.00	.08
1931	88,996	4.80	—
1932	84,697	1,033.64	1.22
1933	91,243	97.50	.10
1934	118,428	1,490.00	1.25
1935	132,970	1,832.00	1.37
1936	230,833	—	—
1937	408,173	12.00	—
1938	480,393	1,041.69	.23
1939	694,302	—	—
TOTAL		5,614.33	

SOURCE: Files of Wisconsin State Banking Department.

In 1931, 1936, 1937 and 1939 the credit unions holding investments in securities had no losses or negligible ones while in only three years, 1932, 1934 and 1935, did the losses reach as much as 1 percent of total investments outstanding at the end of the year. This would appear to be a very successful investment policy, particularly in view of the lack of financial training among most credit union members.

CHAPTER VII

MEMBERS' SHAREHOLDINGS

THE major source of working funds of the credit union is furnished by the purchase of stock in instalments by the membership. These share purchases represent the thrift-promoting function of the credit union and are related to its loan function through pooling the contributions thus made and lending them to borrowing members.

Shares of stock are issued in denominations of $5 per share and can be paid for in full at the time of subscription or in regular weekly or semi-monthly instalments in amounts determined by the members. The money paid in on shares may be withdrawn on any day when payment of shares is made. The directors have the right to require a member at any time to give thirty days' written notice of his intention to withdraw the whole or part of the amount paid in by him; however, many organizations do not enforce this provision. At no time shall more than one-half of the organization's monthly receipts be applied to the payment of withdrawing shares without the consent of the directors. Payments are to be made in the order in which written notices of withdrawal are filed.

In order to determine how effectively credit unions are appealing to people eligible to join, the potential membership, total membership and average members per credit union from 1931 through 1939 is summarized in Table 32. The potential membership figure includes all people in the organization or plant having the credit union. The ratio of total to potential membership increased steadily from 1931-1939, rising from 13 percent in 1931 to 41.7 per cent in 1939. One factor that has tended to keep the ratio down during the period has been the constant addition of new unions. Once an organization is chartered, the potential membership figure is increased by the number of people eligible to join but actual membership increases slowly with the result that the ratio of actual to potential membership is kept down. With the slowing up in the growth of new unions, this ratio will undoubtedly increase.

TABLE 32

ACTUAL AND POTENTIAL MEMBERSHIP IN WISCONSIN CREDIT UNIONS 1931-1939

Year	Potential Membership	Total Membership	Percent Total to Potential Membership	Average Members Per Credit Union
1931	49,240	6,429	13.0	123.6
1932	71,061	10,136	14.3	76.7
1933	121,675	19,470	16.0	96.8
1934	162,452	37,236	22.9	134.4
1935	187,924	57,487	30.6	150.0
1936	235,749	80,284	34.1	176.4
1937	258,865	101,226	39.1	207.4
1938	288,550	117,423	40.7	216.6
1939	319,909	133,504	41.7	237.1

SOURCE: Files of the Wisconsin State Banking Department.

The average number of members (shareholders) has increased over the period, too. Beginning with 1932 the average number per credit union was 76 and rose to 237 in 1939 which was a new high.

TABLE 33

AVERAGE SHAREHOLDINGS WISCONSIN CREDIT UNION MEMBERS 1931-1939

Year	Average Shareholding Per Member
1931	$95.18
1932	79.48
1933	50.63
1934	44.62
1935	46.95
1936	53.05
1937	58.88
1938	58.01
1939	64.09

SOURCE: Files of Wisconsin State Banking Department.

In Table 33 data summarizing the average shareholding per member from 1931 through 1939 are presented. In order to compile this figure dividends credited to shares, reserve for dividends payable and shares outstanding were added and the resultant figure was divided by the number of members. The average shareholding per member was never over $100 in this period. In 1931 the figure was around $95 but fell in subsequent years, reaching a low of $44.62 in 1934. The newly formed credit unions increased the number of their members rapidly and many of these new members had only a few shares or only partly paid shares. Thereafter average shareholdings rose and by 1939 were around $64; if the credit union movement stabilizes in the future the result will probably be further increase in this figure.

It was pointed out earlier that some credit unions have surplus funds when personal loans are not in demand. A number of credit unions in Wisconsin have attempted to cope with this problem. The Statutes do not specify any maximum for individual shareholdings nor is there any ruling by the Commission. Some unions have, however, placed a ceiling on shareholdings per member and the practice is by no means uniform.[1] The Milwaukee Municipal Credit Union stands at one extreme in this respect; it has limited individual shareholdings to a maximum of $10,000 and accumulated dividends, while on the other extreme we find the State Capitol Employees' Credit Union which has a ceiling of $500 and accumulated dividends for an individual member. The other organizations which have resorted to the practice of limiting members' shareholding range in between these extremes.

Limitation upon members' shareholdings is resorted to by the older, larger credit unions that have acquired a substantial amount of surplus cash against which dividends must be paid while there are no adequate investment outlets which enable

1 The ceiling on individual shareholdings may be established by a blanket limitation on the amount of shares purchased or may be achieved by limiting the amount of shares to be acquired in a stated period.

this cash to be converted into earning assets. Furthermore some outlets, namely mortgage loans, are regulated too stringently to enable the organization to use up their entire cash funds.

There are, however, a few newer credit unions that also limit maximum shareholdings of individual members. The motivation in these cases is quite different from that in older unions. Since newer organizations ordinarily have their entire funds invested in loans to members, they try to protect themselves from large withdrawals on shares which might embarrass them should their assets be temporarily frozen, by limiting the amounts they will take from any one person.

Dividends on Share Investments

The Wisconsin Statutes pertaining to credit unions specify the manner in which the amount of earnings available for dividends shall be computed. After the gross earnings have been ascertained and the expenses are deducted, the credit union must set aside the amount required for the guaranty fund. Out of the remainder the board of directors of the union may declare a dividend. Dividends are paid only on *fully paid-up* stock, may be declared annually, semi-annually or quarterly and may be paid in cash or credited to the account of the member in the same manner as payments on shares. While the Statutes do not place any maximum limit on dividend payments, the model set of by-laws provided to these organizations by the Banking Department limits the dividend rate to 6 percent. If a credit union wants to pay a rate in excess of this it must apply to the Commission for special permission. In practice there are very few applications for permission. However, a number of older unions are operating under old by-laws which make no provisions for limitation of dividends, hence may pay any rate they desire. As can be seen from Table 34 very few organizations pay rates in excess of 6 percent.

Dividends are paid on the share month of investment and the following example will illustrate the method of computing.

A person buys one share of stock for $5 on January 1st and dividends are declared semi-annually, namely June 30. This

TABLE 34

DIVIDENDS DECLARED AND SHARES OUTSTANDING WISCONSIN CREDIT UNIONS 1930-1939

Year	Total Dividends Declared (In Dollars)	Total Shares Outstanding At End of Year (In Dollars)	Percentage of Dividends To Shares
1930	$20,399	$421,934	4.8
1931	24,923	590,151	4.2
1932	37,940	778,105	4.9
1933	45,172	966,944	4.7
1934	64,293	1,621,822	4.0
1935	103,081	2,639,388	3.9
1936	159,963	4,142,748	3.8
1937	220,521	5,780,603	3.8
1938	258,933	6,592,538	3.9
1939	316,188	8,286,708	3.8

SOURCE: Files of Wisconsin State Banking Department.

member has held one share for 6 months or 6 share months. Assuming the dividend rate is 4.8 percent per annum, the shareholder earns 2 cents a share a month.[2] Dividends are paid only on the shares outstanding at the end of the period for which they are declared. Thus, a person who has purchased $100 of shares on January 1 and withdrew $90 on May 1 would receive dividends on $10 (2 shares), the amount outstanding on June 30.

Sometimes dividends are not paid at the end of the fiscal period of a credit union's operations (usually December 31) but instead a reserve account, reserve for dividends payable, is set up. The amount thus treated is charged to the current period's earnings and is disbursed in cash or by crediting the amount to the shareholder's investment at the beginning of the succeeding fiscal period. This method of meeting dividends is employed for two reasons: it serves to facilitate the annual audit of members' pass books by the auditing committee as re-

2 $5.00 × .048 = 24 cents. This divided by twelve months would give the monthly share dividend of 2 cents.

quired by the statute, and to stimulate attendance at the annual meeting since there is the prospect of receiving dividends in cash.

Dividends are also paid by crediting the amount of the dividend to the shareholder's account. Since many of the share accounts of credit union members are small, the dividend amounts only to a few cents and it would be very impractical to write a check to meet these payments, hence they are credited to the share account of the members. In this way the organization is also promoting thrift, since the dividends credited are an addition to the accumulated savings of the member. Dividends so credited may subsequently be withdrawn in cash. The final method of meeting dividend payments is to pay the shareholder directly in cash.

The relationship of dividends declared to shares outstanding in Table 34 shows that the ratio decreased during the latter part of the 1930's. It was 4.8 in 1930, fell to 4.2 in 1931, rose again in 1932 to 4.9, then decreased in every year with the exception of 1938 where it stood at 3.8, rose to 3.9 in 1938 and finally fell to 3.8 in 1939. The downward trend is probably exaggerated by the steady growth in the number of credit unions during this period. Since the partially paid shares of new members were included in the total of shares outstanding the denominator of the ratio was exaggerated. This factor led to a slight decline in the ratio, but there were more important reasons accounting for the fall. The decline in money rates after 1931-1932 reduced the credit unions' income from investments as did the increase in its idle cash with the result that dividend payments were reduced somewhat. Another reason for the decline was the deliberate policy of the Banking Department both to preach and compel a more conservative accounting policy. Credit unions were urged to reduce dividend rates; they were often forced to increase their guaranty fund by dipping into net earnings; and the practice of building up the undivided profit account as a buffer for unforeseen contingencies was encouraged.

TABLE 35

DIVIDEND RATE PAID BY WISCONSIN CREDIT UNIONS ON MEMBERS' SHARES DURING 1939

Annual Dividend Rate	All Unions		Unions Chartered on or Before Dec. 31, 1932	
	Number	Percent	Number	Percent
No Dividend	72	13.2	1	1.0
.01 — .99	—	—	—	—
1.00 — 1.99	4	.7	1	1.0
2.00 — 2.99	10	1.8	1	1.0
3.00 — 3.99	53	9.7	7	6.8
4.00 — 4.99	198	36.3	28	27.1
5.00 — 5.99	135	24.7	39	37.8
6.00 — 6.99	72	13.1	25	24.3
7.00 — and over	3	.5	1	1.0
TOTAL	547	100.0	103	100.0

SOURCE: Files of Wisconsin State Banking Department.

Dividends paid on members' shares in 1939 are summarized in Table 35. It was possible to get data for 547 of the 563 organizations in existence at the end of 1939. Around 13 percent of all unions reported no dividends in that year. Most of the unions falling into the group were either newly formed organizations which had not yet developed a sufficient volume of business to pay a dividend or older, inactive organizations which, in the process of liquidating, submitted an annual report on operations during the year. About 2.5 percent of the number paid dividends ranging between 1.00 and 2.99 percent, while approximately 10 percent paid dividends of 3.00 to 3.99 percent.

Almost three-fourths of the credit unions paid out dividends of 4.00 percent or more, and the most common rate falls between 4.00 and 4.99 percent. Most of the cases in this class were 4.8 percent and the main reason for the frequency of this rate is the ease with which the dividend can be computed.[3]

3 A dividend rate of 4.8 percent is 2 cents a share month, hence the amount of computation and bookkeeping is kept to a minimum.

About one-fourth of the unions paid dividends of 5.00 to 5.99 percent, with a bi-modal occurrence of 5.0 and 5.5 percent accounting for most of the cases in this group. About 13 percent of the unions paid dividends of 6.00 to 6.99 percent with most of the cases falling at 6 percent which also is easily computed.[4] Less than 1 percent of the unions paid dividends of 7.00 percent or over, with the highest rate reaching 8.6 percent.

In order to examine the relationship between the rate of dividend paid and the size of the credit union, the distribution of dividends for those credit unions chartered on or before December 31, 1932, was computed; they were 103 in number. As was shown above[5] in a general way there is a relationship between size of assets and age. It is evident from Table 35 that age and size do affect the dividend rate paid. Only 1 percent of the "old" credit unions reported no dividend paid while 13 percent of all unions fell into this category. For dividend rates ranging from 1.00 to 4.99 percent a higher frequency of occurrence among all credit unions was found than among those chartered on or before December 31, 1932. Beginning with dividends of 5.0 percent or more, however, the trend is reversed and the frequency of occurrence is greater for the older unions than for all unions. The modal dividend rate for the old unions falls in the 5.00 to 5.99 percent category while it is the 4.00 to 4.99 percent class for all unions. Three-fourths of all unions paid dividends in the 4.00 to 6.99 range, and about nine-tenths of the old unions were found in this range.

4 Two and one-half cents per share month.

5 See pp. 44-45.

CHAPTER VIII

EARNINGS AND EXPENSES

It is generally agreed that the expenses of operating a credit union are low, especially when compared with the expenses of commercial lenders such as small loan companies, industrial banks and personal loan departments of commercial banks. In this section the components of expense and income in relation to average loans outstanding will be analyzed; finally a breakdown of the type of expenses incurred by unions of different size will be presented.

The Statute regulating credit union operations and the model by-laws specify the maximum expenses that may be incurred by these organizations. The board of directors cannot receive any compensation for their services as members of the board but the officers and credit committee may receive such compensation as the board authorizes. All expenses must be paid from earnings. In no case can the credit union pay or become liable to pay in the course of any fiscal or calendar year sums of money in excess of one-half its gross earnings. These expenses cover the following items: salaries, fees or other compensation to officers, directors, auditors, all other employees, rent, advertising, printing, stationery, bonds, examining loans and abstracts, commissions and all other operating expenses.

A credit union with an accumulated capital of less than $2,500 is exempted from the above limitation but in no case shall its annual operating expense exceed $100. The provision relating to organizations under $2,500 was put into the statute in 1935 in order to enable small organizations to continue in business without violating the law. Previously numerous small credit unions exceeded the maximum permitted by law in meeting the indispensable expenses of bonding their treasurer and paying the assessment fee to the Banking Department. The general idea behind limitation of expense and the prohibition against receipt of payment by the directors is to prevent the credit union from being run for the profit of a few individuals.

Total expenses are composed of salaries, interest on notes payable, rent, commissions and other expenses. The expense item, salaries, comprises the largest percent of total expenses, and includes salaries given to paid employees, officers, etc. In 1929 it accounted for about 65 percent of total expenses; thereafter it fell, reaching 47 percent in 1932 and hovered around this point through 1939. This behavior is a little surprising because one would expect that as credit unions get older and larger they would be able to pay certain officers who did not receive compensation for their services when the organization was small. Moreover, as the unions grow in size we would expect them to hire paid employes, an expense they could not afford before. That the proportion of expense consisting of salaries does not increase is probably due to the fact that many new credit unions were chartered which did not pay any salaries but had to meet other expenses. The result is that the proportion of salaries to total expenses declined, while in 1929, 1930 and 1931 the few unions that there were had been in existence for a period of years and were hiring paid employees. The salary item represents an understatement of the true amount of this expense because some credit unions report part, and in some cases, all their salary expense in the other expense item. In addition the expense, commissions, usually represents the compensations paid to the treasurer which is a salary item in reality. In order to avoid contracting a fixed expense a few credit unions compensate the treasurer on the basis of a fixed percent of interest income or a stated number of cents for each borrower, thereby relating the treasurer's salary to the volume of business done. Some small portion of the commission expense represents commissions paid on securities purchased. In order to get a true picture of the salary expense, we should break down the commission expense and obtain the amount of this which is paid to treasurers, then compute that part of other expense which consists of salaries and add these two items to the reported salary expense. Since this is not possible the salary item is understated.

Interest on notes payable varies with the volume of borrowing by credit unions. The proportion of total expenses accounted for by interest on borrowed funds has never been very large, and the relative importance of this item has varied over the period 1929 through 1939. It was about 4.5 in 1929 and increased to a high of 9 percent at the depth of the depression when credit unions increased their borrowing upon finding themselves in difficulty and thereafter declined to around 1.5 percent of total expenses.

There are very few credit unions that pay rent for the space they occupy. Several of the very large organizations incur this expense. In 1929, 1930 and 1931 rent comprised around 2.5 percent of total expenses. Thereafter, many new unions were formed which do not pay rent with the result that the portion of total expenses consisting of rent has declined to less than 1 percent of total expenses. It may be expected that in the future with fewer and fewer new organizations being chartered and the older unions growing larger, rent will loom larger as a percent of total expenses.

As was mentioned above, the item, other expenses, is a hodge-podge of various expenses which can not be segregated. Included in this item is the premium paid on fidelity bonds, some salaries, the annual fees paid to the Banking Commission, advertising, stationery and supplies, dues paid to the Wisconsin Credit Union League, the premiums paid on loan and share insurance and a few miscellaneous expenses. The other expenses item has risen from around 28 percent of total expenses to around 50 percent of total expenses over the period.

In order to get some idea of the relationship of expenses to loans the ratio of gross expenses to average loan balances outstanding,[1] was computed from 1929 through 1939 (Table 36). It stood at 2.8 in 1929 and thereafter ranged from 2.0 to 2.4 until 1936. The decline is probably accounted for by the large increase in new unions which were making many loans

1 Average of loan balances outstanding at the beginning and end of the year.

TABLE 36

EARNINGS AND EXPENSES OF WISCONSIN CREDIT UNIONS 1929-1939

Year	Average All Loans Outstanding	Ratio Gross Earnings to All Loans Outstanding	Ratio Gross Expense to All Loans Outstanding
1929	$232,990	11.4	2.8
1930	354,935	11.2	2.4
1931	484,636	10.9	2.0
1932	649,291	10.8	2.3
1933	834,976	10.8	2.0
1934	1,206,182	10.5	2.0
1935	1,932,837	10.9	2.3
1936	3,020,556	10.8	2.4
1937	4,360,499	11.3	2.9
1938	5,572,607	10.8	3.1
1939	6,592,854	10.8	3.3

SOURCE: Files of Wisconsin State Banking Department.

but were too young and small to have started paying salaries to officers and hired employees. Beginning with 1937 the gross expense ratio rose and in 1939 was equal to 3.3 percent of average loans outstanding. The increase was partly due to the falling off in the rate at which new credit unions were formed which meant that the increase in loan balances was accounted for mainly by the older credit unions who were paying officers and hiring paid employees. Furthermore, in the late thirties more credit unions were taking out borrower life insurance which was paid by the credit union and not by the borrower, hence adding to gross expenses.

Despite the increase in the gross expense ratio in the late thirties credit union expenses were very low, especially in comparison with the expenses of commercial organizations making loans to consumers. To take one example, total expenses[2] of

2 Includes salaries, bad debts, advertising, taxes and license fees, rent, printing, stationery, postage, travel, legal fees, auditing, depreciation of furniture and fixtures, insurance, recording and acknowledging fees and sundry other expenses.

Wisconsin small loan companies in 1939 were about 14.5 percent of "average employed assets." [3] The reason is that credit union officials normally give their services free of charge or receive only nominal compensation, while other usual commercial expenses like rent are non-existent, because of a subsidy by the sponsoring organization. Because of the common bond among members, the expense and effort required to investigate loan applicants, check security and follow collections is less than for commercial organizations.

Gross earnings consist of interest income on loans, entrance fees, fines, other fees and miscellaneous, premium on loans and profits on withdrawals. Interest income on personal loans, mortgage loans, investments and notes receivable accounts for the major source of gross earnings of credit unions. In 1929 this item amounted to 86 percent of gross earnings and in 1939 it was 96 percent.

Entrance fees are charged new members to reimburse the organization for the expense of setting up the ledger account and issuing a pass book. It is obvious that the relative importance of entrance fees as a source of gross earnings is primarily determined by the number of new credit unions formed as this in the main determines new credit union members who will pay these entrance fees. This item comprised about 2.4 percent of gross earnings in 1929 and rose to 4.1 percent in 1934 and fell thereafter, being 1.0 percent in 1939. It is reasonable to expect an even further decline in its relative importance as a source of gross earnings since the rate of credit union growth is decreasing.

Fines are charged on accounts that are delinquent in meeting payments as agreed in the loan contract. The objective of this penalty is to prevent delinquencies by charging for such failure to meet contractual obligations. Fines were never an important source of earnings, amounting to only about 2.3 percent of

3 Computed by multiplying the average of net loan balances (loan balances minus reserve for bad debts) outstanding at the beginning and at the end of the year by 1.15.

gross earnings in 1929. Since that time they have become even less important and were less than .6 of 1 percent in 1939. Many of the credit unions have discontinued the practice of assessing a fine on delinquent accounts, because a borrower, upon payment of the fine because of delinquency felt that he had paid for this privilege and was therefore entitled to continue his delinquency. Since the original purpose of fines, namely to prevent delinquency, has had the opposite effect, many organizations have ceased charging fines and insist on being paid promptly.

Profit on withdrawals is an unimportant source of earnings and relates only to mortgage loans. Some older credit unions made a sinking fund type of mortgage loan where an individual purchased shares on which he made payments each month. At the end of the period the dividends credited and the money paid on the shares was applied to the loan which was then paid up. Let us assume at the end of five years the borrower had $1,500 in the share account, consisting of $1,200 paid in on shares and $300 in dividends credited, and the borrower was delinquent. If he refinanced the loan the credit union charged a renewal fee of 10 percent of dividends credited on the shares. These $30 would be classed as earnings and called profit on withdrawal. Premium loans are also an unimportant source of gross earnings and are accounted for by a handful of organizations. These few unions make mortgage loans and personal loans at a figure below the rate charged by other unions but charge a privilege fee for the practice. Thus a union will make a mortgage loan for $1,000 at 5 percent which is 1 percent less than the ordinary rate. In order to get this loan the borrower must pay a premium of 1 percent or $10 and this sum is entered as an earning. Other fees and miscellaneous items consist of dividends on insurance premiums paid, income from rental of real estate owned, etc.

The ratio of gross earnings to average loans outstanding has been fairly constant from 1929 through 1939 ranging from about 10.5 to 11.4 percent.

Gross income for small loan companies in Wisconsin in 1939 was much higher, being about 23.4 percent of "average employed assets." Thus expenses and gross income of credit unions were both lower than these items for small loan companies.

In order to discover whether the larger credit unions were more efficient than the smaller ones a frequency distribution was compiled which cross-classified organizations by size of assets and the ratio of total expenses to gross earnings (Table 37). From an examination of the table it is apparent that the

TABLE 37

EARNINGS AND EXPENSES OF WISCONSIN CREDIT UNIONS, CLASSIFIED BY SIZE, 1939

Size of Credit Union (Volume of assets)	Number of Unions	Gross Earnings	Gross Expenses	Percent Expenses To Earnings
$1 — $2,499.99	160	$13,529	$5,170	38.3
2,500 — 4,999.99	106	31,686	9,967	31.4
5,000 — 9,999.99	101	57,648	17,859	30.9
10,000 — 24,999.99	118	142,876	45,342	31.0
25,000 — 49,999.99	39	113,085	33,442	29.5
50,000 — 99,999.99	16	94,735	29,841	31.5
Over 100,000	16	263,355	77,739	29.5
TOTAL	556	$716,914	$219,360	30.5

SOURCE: Files of Wisconsin State Banking Department.

smaller credit unions are the least efficient. The ratio of expense to gross earnings for these unions is over 38 percent. The reason for this probably is accounted for by the fact that most of the costs of operation are relatively fixed so that a larger volume of business up to a point will not lead to added costs. Thus we find that as the size of credit union increases to over $2,500 in assets the expense to gross earnings ratio declines to 31.4 percent. Beyond this size, however, there is no evidence to substantiate any assertion that the larger the credit union the more efficient it becomes. Credit unions having from $2,500 to over $100,000 in assets all have an expense to earnings ratio around 30 percent. What probably happens as the size of credit union increases is that new expenses for paid personnel, etc., also increase but that the increased absolute amount of expense is offset by a corresponding increase in the volume of business accommodated so that the ratio of expenses to gross earnings remains about the same.

CHAPTER IX*

LIQUIDATIONS OF CREDIT UNIONS

ONE of the criticisms leveled against the credit union movement is the high "failure" rate among these institutions. Before discussing the statistical information, it is necessary to clear up some terminological difficulties as well as to explain the process of liquidation as dictated by the Wisconsin statutes. The use of the term "failure" to describe a liquidation of a credit union is not only incorrect but is also invidious since it implies an insufficiency to discharge all debt enforceable against it which is presumably borne by the share-holders of the "failed" credit union. The term "liquidation" shall be used in the technical sense in which it should correctly be employed.

At the time a credit union is organized and approved by the state Banking Department, it receives a charter from the state, granting it a corporate existence. When it ceases to function it must apply to the Banking Department and then to the state for cancellation of its charter to avoid any future liabilities. The process of *charter cancellation is called liquidation* and this is the only meaning which may correctly be attached to liquidations in regard to Wisconsin credit unions.

The laws of Wisconsin provide for two types of liquidation, namely *voluntary* and *involuntary*. The procedure involved in a voluntary liquidation is relatively simple. At a meeting specially called to consider the subject, upon the unanimous recommendation of the board of directors, the members may vote to dissolve the corporation, provided that at least two-thirds of the members are present at the meeting and provided further that not more than ten members, either in person or by written notice, object to the dissolution. A committee of three is elected to liquidate the assets of the credit union,[1] and place the resulting funds in a local bank. No accounts can be withdrawn

* Reproduced with minor changes from *Journal of Business of the University of Chicago,* No. 2, April, 1946 with permission of the editor.

1 The members of this committee must be bonded to prevent losses through embezzlement or fraud.

until all the funds are collected, although a liquidating dividend may be distributed. After all the debts have been paid, the remainder of the funds is then pro-rated on each share of stock, according to the amount paid on this stock. Once all the funds have been disbursed, the credit union sends its resolution of dissolution papers to the Banking Department which passes it on to the State Department where the charter is cancelled.[2]

The procedure involved in an involuntary liquidation is more complicated. Under the Wisconsin statutes,[3] the Banking Commission may take possession and control of the business and property of any credit union when it finds that the credit union:

1. Is conducting business contrary to law.
2. Has violated its charter or any law.
3. Is conducting its business in an unauthorized or unsafe manner.
4. Is in an unsound or unsafe condition to transact its business.
5. Has an impairment of its capital.
6. Cannot with safety and expedience continue business.
7. Has suspended payments of its obligations.
8. Has neglected or refused to comply with the terms of an order of the Commission.

Upon taking possession of the business and property of the credit union, the Banking Commission serves notice upon the president and secretary of the organization, informing them of its act. Thereupon, notice must be given to any individual or association known to the Banking Commission, to be in possession of any assets of said organization. In order to assist in the liquidation and distribution of the assets of the credit union, the Banking Commission may appoint one or more special

2 Laws of Wisconsin, 1939, Chapter 186.18.

3 Laws of Wisconsin, 1937, Chapter 215.33.

deputy commissioners, employ such counsel and procure whatever expert assistance is required and may also retain such officers and employees of the organization as are deemed necssary. These men shall furnish the security for the faithful discharge of their duties the Banking Commission deems proper.

The special deputy commissioner can make delivery on all deeds and titles necessary and proper to effect any sale an transfer of property of the credit union after approval is granted by the Banking Commission and the circuit court of the county in which the credit union is located. After taking possession of the property and business of the credit union, the commissioner is authorized to collect all money due the organization and do anything else needed to conserve its assets and business and to liquidate its affairs. He must advertise, calling on all persons having claims against the union to present these claims and he can then reject or approve them. Any interested party can file objections to the claim and if these objections are valid, the claims can be disallowed. An inventory of assets must be drawn up by the commissioner and at the expiration of the time allowed for claims, he must present a list of claims specifying those he rejects. Next, the Commission must collect all debts due the credit union and claims it holds. The withdrawal value of shares pledged on a loan by the credit union shall be applied and credited to the loan and the borrower is liable only for the balance. The compensation of the individuals involved in the liquidation plus the expenses of liquidation itself shall be paid out of the resources of the credit union. After all the expenses and debts are paid off, the surplus, if there is any, can be used to pay one or more dividends. At any time after the end of the year following the first notice to creditors, a final dividend may be declared. If, upon payment of expenses and debts, there are not sufficient funds to pay shareholders in full, the book value of each member's holdings is reduced proportionately.

Credit unions which voluntarily cease business generally handle the liquidation themselves through a special committee although there are several instances of voluntary liquidations where an outside liquidator has been appointed by the Banking Department or where the Department itself has handled the liquidation. When an involuntary liquidation takes place, the Banking Department, through a specially appointed commission takes charge of the proceedings. The Banking Department prefers a voluntary to an involuntary liquidation, since in the latter case the expenses are higher. For this reason most credit unions elect voluntary liquidation even though the initial compulsion to close down may come from the Department itself.

The term " involuntary " need not be one of opprobrium since the Banking Department may close the organization with a view to serving the best interests of the shareholders or creditors in preventing the union from operating.[4] It seems extremely difficult and perhaps too subjective to attempt to reclassify voluntary into involuntary liquidations in those cases where there is evidence of compulsion by the Banking Department to get the union to close. From an examination of the correspondence of the liquidating credit unions, these organizations frequently are in the process of going out of business and the Department merely uses "compulsion" by giving the officers directions as to the correct procedure.[5]

Recognizing the limitations attached to the meaning of voluntary and involuntary as applied by the Banking Commission, we find that of the 91 credit unions liquidated in Wisconsin from January 1, 1923 through June 30, 1940, only *one* case represented an involuntary liquidation.

As was pointed out earlier, the credit union movement grew very slowly in Wisconsin until 1931; there were only 22 organizations in existence at the end of 1930. Beginning with

4 F. E. Wilcox, *op cit.*, p. 65.

5 There are several instances where the credit union is not doing business and is informally liquidating. If it were to pay withdrawals in full, it might mean that those individuals who are last to demand their funds might not be able to get any. To prevent this contingency from arising the Banking Department brings pressure to bear by preventing payments on withdrawals unless the procedure outlined by the Statutes is followed.

1931, the year a state-paid credit union organizer was added to the state Banking Department, the growth in numbers has been extremely vigorous. From 1923 through June 30, 1940, 667 organizations received charters to do business. For many years the handful of unions that were chartered experienced no liquidations so that the growth was merely a product of new unions. The first liquidation of a credit union took place in 1931 and this was multiplied in the ensuing years so that by June 30, 1940, 91 liquidations had occurred. The number of organizations ceasing business constituted about 13 percent of the total number of credit unions formed (Table 38).

TABLE 38

NUMBER OF WISCONSIN CREDIT UNIONS BEGINNING BUSINESS, STARTING LIQUIDATION, AND STILL ACTIVE, BY YEARS, 1923 THROUGH JUNE 30, 1940: CLASSIFIED BY YEAR OPENED

In order to get some idea of the relationsship of expenses

Year	Beginning Business during the year	Starting liquidation during year	In business at end of year	Credit Unions in existence June 30, 1940 and year opened: Number remaining	Percent of Original Number
1923	2	..	2	2	100.0
1924	..	..	2	..	....
1925	..	..	2	..	....
1926	..	..	2	..	....
1927	4	..	6	3	75.0
1928	4	..	10	4	100.0
1929	3	..	13	1	33.3
1930	9	..	22	7	78.0
1931	31	1	52	24	77.5
1932	80	..	132	62	77.5
1933	79	10	201	73	97.4
1934	83	7	277	69	83.2
1935	109	3	383	92	84.5
1936	82	10	455	73	89.1
1937	52	19	488	45	86.6
1938	64	10	542	61	95.4
1939	46	25	563	41	89.2
1940[a]	19	6	576	19	100.0
TOTAL ..	667	91		576	86.3%

[a] Covers period from January 1 through June 30, 1940.
SOURCE: Files of Wisconsin State Banking Department.

In order to compare the mortality rate among Wisconsin state credit unions with that in some other states, the ratio was taken of New York state credit unions liquidated to the total number of unions formed from 1914 through 1937, and of Massachusetts state credit unions from 1910 through 1937. The figures are 42 percent[6] for New York and 37 percent for Massachusetts[7] while the ratio of credit unions liquidated to credit unions formed in Wisconsin from 1923 through 1939 is only 13 percent or one third the others. Since these figures cover varying periods, the mortality rates for these three states were computed for comparable periods — the years 1923 through 1937. The rate for New York is 64 percent; for Massachusetts 40 percent; and only 9 percent for Wisconsin. While these figures reflect very favorably upon the vitality and organizational success of Wisconsin state credit unions relative to state credit unions in Massachusetts and New York, there were very special circumstances in both states that served to magnify the mortality rate. The credit union movement in New York showed a heavy mortality rate because of the large number of "open" credit unions that were permitted during the twenties; this type of membership is notorious for its inability to survive for long periods of time. In Massachusetts, an amendment to the credit union law in 1926 compelled all persons or associations doing business in the manner of a credit union to secure a credit union charter. Many of these were granted charters when they applied to the Banking Department and because the charters were granted too leniently, subsequently closed very rapidly.[8]

6 F. E. Wilcox, *op. cit.*, p. 66.

7 The figures for Massachusetts were computed from J. L. Snider, *op. cit.*, p. 27. In order to make the data comparable, however, it was necessary to exclude the Federal Credit Unions which are included in his figures. Furthermore, we figure 16 liquidations in 1937 while his total is only 9.

8 The Bank Commissioner in his report for 1926 estimated that 156 such associations were granted charters during that year. See J. L. Snider, *op. cit.*, p. 29.

While the liquidation experience for Wisconsin credit unions shows a much more favorable picture than for New York and Massachusetts, it must be borne in mind that the Wisconsin unions have not experienced a major depression. There were only ten organizations in existence in Wisconsin at the end of 1928 and in fact the credit union movement had not really started. By the end of 1928 there were 297 organizations in Massachusetts[9] and 112 in New York[10] and they had to contend with the deflation consequent upon the depression after 1929. It will therefore be interesting to observe the experience undergone by Wisconsin organizations when, as, and if a major depression like that following 1929 occurs.

The first credit union liquidation came in 1931; in 1932 there were no closings but subsequently there were closings in every year. The heaviest concentration of liquidations took place in 1933 and after, but only in 1937 and 1939 did the ratio of credit unions liquidating to credit unions formed in the same year rise above 20 percent, the figures being 36 and 54 percent respectively. The ratio of liquidations to charter grantings rose from 12 percent in 1936 to 36 percent in 1937, fell to 16 percent in 1938 and rose to 54 percent in 1939.

In column four of Table 38 is shown the number of organizations existing on June 30, 1940 out of the number formed in a given year. These are expressed in percentage form in the fifth column. Only one-third of the unions formed in 1929 are still active while in no other case does the percentage of unions formed still existing fall below 75 percent. One hundred percent of the unions formed in 1928 are still active. The percentage of unions formed in '27, '30, '31, and '32 which are still active ranges from 75 to 78, while the ratios for '34, '35, '36, '37 and '39 range from 83 to 89; for 1933 and 1938 the figures range from 94 to 95 percent.

9 See J. L. Snider, *op. cit.*, p. 27.

10 See F. E. Wilcox, *op. cit.*, p. 66.

Reason for Closing

There is no one clear-cut reason for liquidation; by resorting to more than one source of information it was possible to obtain not only the primary and secondary cause but in some instances, tertiary reasons for closing.

Of the 91 unions that were liquidated through June 1940, 46 credit unions (50 percent) were closed because of a lack of interest among the members of the organization usually manifesting itself in an unsatisfactory volume of loans or members, or both. In about a quarter of these cases a lack of interest characterizes the credit union before it is even started, although it has received a charter from the state so that only 35 of the 46 liquidating unions ever did any business. The 9 unions which were liquidated without ever transacting business and the 2 unions whose charters were revoked, were straight cases of no interest among members or potential members. In addition, there are 18 cases where the unions did conduct business but they, too, are clearly characterized by a lack of interest among members or potential members. Of the remaining 17 liquidations, the contributory causes in 5 cases were small size; poor management accounts for 8 cases; reduced employment accounts for 2 liquidations, while spreading the organization over a wide area [11] accounts for 2 unions. Four of the 5 cases of smallness impress one with the fact that in view of the fewness even of the potential membership, the liquidation could have been avoided by refusing to have permitted the organization to be formed. While the fifth union potentially had enough members, they were scattered over a wide area.

Poor management accounts for 13 liquidations or 14 percent of the total number; the lack of management manifests itself in a number of ways. The union may be extending unsatisfactory loans, it may not be "selling" its loan services to members, it may not be stirring the interest of potential mem-

11 A credit union may be established with a view to caring for the needs of four or five townships which by virtue of their geographical distance does not facilitate effective operation.

TABLE 39

WISCONSIN CREDIT UNIONS LIQUIDATED FROM 1923 THROUGH JUNE 30, 1940 CLASSIFIED BY REASON FOR CLOSING[a]

	Unions doing business[b]	Unions never transacting any business[c]	Charter revoked before operations[d]	Total
No interest and/or unsatisfactory vol. of business	35	9	2	46
Poor Management	13	..	..	13
Depression in plant where credit union is established	20[e]	..	1	21
Embezzlement	5[f]	..	..	5
Company opposition	3	..	..	3
Labor trouble in plant	3	..	..	3
TOTALS	79	9	3	91

[a] Primary reason only. For discussion of this point see text pp. 140ff.

[b] If a credit union has received any payments on shares it is considered to have "done business." Thus some unions which have never extended any loans, are considered to have done business.

[c] A union which has not received any payments on shares by members is considered to have never done any business. In this category, however, there are some organizations that have received entrance fees from members and have purchased supplies. There are a few instances where such credit unions have even incurred very nominal losses upon liquidation since the sale of assets did not provide enough to cover the claims of creditors.

[d] A charter revocation differs from a voluntary liquidation since in the former the organization has no assets.

[e] Includes 2 credit unions which consolidated with other unions.

[f] Includes 1 credit union which consolidated with another union.

SOURCE: Files of Wisconsin State Banking Department. For additional information see text, pp. 140ff.

bers and it may cause suspicion and fears for the organization's safety in the eyes of members or potential members by an unsatisfactory managerial role. The management of the credit union itself may not be interested in the organization and may not call for or attend meetings which, in turn, serves to magnify the apathy of the membership. In dealing with secondary causes of liquidation, 6 of the 13 unions liquidating because of poor management showed no interest on the part of actual or potential members. This is not surprising since poor or inactive management is passed on to members in the form of apathy toward the organization. In one case, reduced employment served to bring about liquidation of the credit union while in the 6 remaining cases poor management is very clearly the sole cause. In one of these credit unions the management was so indolent in its functions that the employer in whose plant the union was organized had to run both his plant and the credit union.[12]

A depression in the plant where the credit union is established accounts for 21 liquidations—23 percent of the number. Breaking down this generality, 6 credit unions were liquidated when the plant in which they were organized was split into several plants, no one of which was large enough to warrant a separate credit union. In 10 cases, the plant closed down completely while in 5 cases the plant reduced operations and laid off many workers or reduced their work week.[13]

An unbiased scrutiny of the liquidation record of these 21 organizations impresses one with the lack of meaning that liquidation figures offer. The credit union is set up in a plant which is doing business, hiring employees and disbursing income in the form of wages. If the plant is split into small plants, causing the union to liquidate because of the unsatisfactory volume of business that can be transacted, the credit unions or the credit union movement should not be condemned. When the base of credit union operations is removed it is inevitable that the organization disappear. The same is true for liquidations resulting from a shut-down of the plant or a substantial

12 In another case, the president of the credit union was a major contributor to the organization's capital and he was interested in running the union in order to maximize his dividend returns even if this was accomplished at the expense of all other members.

13 In one case the credit union received its charter but the plant reduced employment so substantially that the organization never conducted any business.

reduction in the amount of employment offered laborers. These liquidations are, in the final analysis, the result of the operations of the economic system and not the credit union movement. If there are no losses incurred by creditors or shareholders, then the credit unions are to be praised for their attempts to cope by cooperative efforts with a pressing problem of low income groups, namely, lack of credit facilities.

The assets of 2 of the 6 credit unions liquidated when the plant in which they were established was broken up, were sold to credit unions in other branches of the plant where the employees of the dissolved plants were reemployed. In a third case the credit union was consolidated with the credit union in the remaining plant of the company. Thus, 3 of the 6 cases were merely nominal liquidations in that the credit union continued to operate under a new organization or name but the liquidation was made necessary to cancel the charter of the old credit union. In a fourth case, the main part of the plant was given up; hence the credit union lost so many of its actual and potential members that it could no longer function.

Of the 10 credit unions liquidated when the plant in which they were located shut down, 6 ceased functioning. In 2 cases, the credit unions were consolidated with other credit unions and a charter cancellation (liquidation) was necessary but actually those unions continued to function albeit under a new name. Of the remaining 2, we find that the plant eventually reopened, but the members were suspicious of the credit union because it had not functioned during the plant shut-down; hence liquidation was really the result of non-interest among members and/or potential members. One credit union which was liquidated when the plant shut down subsequently took out a new charter when the plant was reopened some years later in 1939.

One of the 5 credit unions which were liquidated because of reduced employment in the plant where they were established never did any business and is therefore a "nominal" liquidation. Three of the 4 other credit unions clearly were liquidated as a result of reduced employment in the plant while lack of interest served as a contributing factor to cause liquidation of the fourth organization.

Strictly speaking, embezzlement is never the actual cause of liquidation of credit unions in Wisconsin because the officers and management who come in contact with the organization's funds are required to be bonded to assure safe conduct of their business. When a defalcation takes place, the bonding company must make good the loss with the result that the funds are restored to the union. The reason for including embezzlement under the primary causes in the 5 cases where such an act did lead to liquidation lies in the fact that the Banking Department "bears down" more heavily on such organizations than on others. One credit union was consolidated with another union in the same plant and to all intents and purposes the organization *had not* ceased business although it was necessary to cancel its charter. In all cases of defalcation poor management can be considered as a secondary cause; in one credit union reduced employment and in another no interest is given as secondary cause of liquidation.

Three credit unions were liquidated as a result of company opposition and in all 3 cases poor management was a strong secondary cause for liquidation. By virtue of their very inadequate management, these unions aroused the suspicions of the employers who feared a liquidation with subsequent losses to members would cause ill-will among employees.

Of the 3 credit unions which were liquidated because of labor trouble in the plant, 2 were forced to liquidate as a result of the terms of the strike settlement. In both cases not many of the striking employees were reinstated, with the resultant decline in the membership, while in the third credit union, there was a jurisdictional dispute which led to jealousy on both sides, with the result that membership in the credit union declined since one labor union felt that the credit union was closely affiliated with the rival trade union and compelled its members to refrain from affiliating themselves with the credit union.

Age of Credit Unions Liquidating

The age of the unions cancelling charters was compiled from the annual reports of the credit unions and is computed from the time elapsing between the date the charter was issued and the date the members voted to dissolve the organization. In almost all cases the age of the credit union is overstated because liquidation almost always commences long before the membership is called upon to vote formally to dissolve. A better idea of the age of the organization would be derived by discovering when the members felt like giving up. Such data, however, are impossible to obtain in most cases and in lieu of it the dissolution date was used as the terminal point in computing age.

Approximately one-half the liquidated organizations were two years of age or less while 83 percent were four years or under. For the most part, decisions to liquidate come fairly early in the credit union's life. There is apparently a period of about two years needed for the credit union to gestate; if the interest of the members still exists after this initial period, then the probability is that, other things being equal, the organization will continue to function. The heavy mortality rate in its youth can be easily understood. In the full blush of organizational campaigns and "pep" talks by a few active participants, the members are aroused. The credit union is novel and like many other novelties attracts the gregarious nature of man; add to this, of course, the prospects of getting loans to a group of impecunious individuals. They think that once the credit union is opened they will immediately be able to borrow. When they realize, however, that the loan funds must be built up by shares purchased by members, themselves, their interest wanes very sharply.

Other things are not, however, equal, so that the older a credit union, the more obstacles are in its way to permanent existence. It would appear that the longer a credit union is in business, the more susceptible it is to changes in underlying economic conditions. Thus an organization started in a period

TABLE 40

CREDIT UNIONS LIQUIDATED IN WISCONSIN FROM 1923 THROUGH JUNE 30, 1940 BY AGE AT TIME DISSOLUTION WAS VOTED

Age of Credit Union	Number of Credit Unions	Percent of Total
6 months and Under	6	6.6
Over 6 months through 1 year	7	7.7
Over 1 year through 1½ years	16	17.6
Over 1½ years through 2 years	17	18.7
Over 2 years through 2½ years	7	7.7
Over 2½ years through 3 years	8	8.8
Over 3 years through 3½ years	3	3.3
Over 3½ years through 4 years	12	13.2
Over 4 years	15	16.4
TOTAL	91	100.0

SOURCE: Files of Wisconsin State Banking Department.

of prosperity, if it lasts long enough, is subject to plant movements, plant closings due to a depression, and other cyclical and secular changes in our economy. In order to test the hypothesis that age makes the credit union susceptible to cyclical, secular and random factors which are not as operative in the case of young organizations, the 30 unions that were three years or over at liquidation were classified by reason for closing and the results compared with the reasons for closing for all liquidated unions. There is some evidence to substantiate the hypothesis although not too conclusively. No interest accounts for 36 percent of the cases of unions three years or older which is lower than for all 91 liquidated unions while poor management accounts for 16 percent which is slightly more than for all unions. Depression in plant only shows as great a percentage for the 30 unions as for all unions. This weakens our hypothesis, for we would expect the evidence to show a higher frequency of occurrence for the organizations three years or over. Embezzlement and company opposition run higher than for all unions while labor trouble is the same for the " old " as for all liquidated unions. Frequently, in the credit union, as in other cooperative ventures, disputes arise between cliques which develop in that organization. The longer an organization exists, the more opportunity is provided for such disputes to arise.

Breaking down the figures on age of liquidated credit unions, to get the average age of these unions by type of membership, the following information was obtained. Among associational credit unions, the average age of the parish credit unions liquidated is 49 months; this figure is overstated by an extreme case of one organization which lasted nine years and one month. If this case is excluded the average life span per liquidated parish credit union is only 39 months; this age is relatively longer than any other type of membership and can probably be explained by the stabilizing influence which the parish priest plays in keeping the organization going. The average age of liquidated farm cooperative credit unions is 24½ months while the figure for other cooperatives is 26 months. The average age of liquidated labor union credit unions is 27 months and for miscellaneous [14] associational credit unions, 15½ months.

Among the residential "open" credit unions, the average age of the liquidated organization is 38 months. This figure, like that for parish credit unions, is distorted by the inclusion of one union whose life span is ten years and eight months. If this case is excluded, the average life is brought down to 23 months. The average life of the occupational credit unions was 32½ months. On the average, residential and associational credit unions have about the same life span whereas occupational organizations have a more protracted life span.

There is one general observation which can be drawn from the examination of the age of liquidated organizations which may serve as a suggestion to promotional and administrative units in the credit union field. The critical period in credit union development and certainly one field where the adminis-

14 Includes American Legion, Professional Club, Negro group and fraternal society.

trative organizations can aid growth[15] is in the early stages of development. From the correspondence of credit unions, from the comments of state Banking Department employees and from discussions with people active in the credit union movement, it is clear that the government agency in charge of these organizations would eliminate a substantial number of liquidations at an early age if it could send an advisor or examiner to explain the operations of the business and to render advice periodically, when requested. It is truly pathetic to read the pleas of a group of self-respecting people who, while ignorant in the field of finance, want to set up a cooperative agency to assist themselves. If their requests for advice were attended to promptly and if they were examined frequently and their errors rectified at an early date, their interest would certainly not wane, nor would the number of credit unions liquidated in the early stages of life be as great.

Size of Liquidating Unions

The data on assets of the liquidated unions at the latest date prior to dissolution is voted by the membership, are obtained from the annual or semi-annual reports of individual unions (Table 41). These figures contain a bias which understates the size of assets. The credit union may be in the throes of liquidation long before the membership votes to dissolve, hence the figures will understate the size of these organizations since they are taken at a date near the termination of the credit union's life; the most accurate method of obtaining these figures would be to take the figures at the time the union decides to liquidate rather than the time when they vote to dissolve. In most of the cases it is impossible to get such information, hence it was necessary to resort to the procedure followed above. Where it was possible to get information on assets at the time liquidation started, it was used.

15 No administrative or promotional organization in the credit union movement can do much about unemployment or cyclical and secular variations in business activity.

TABLE 41

CREDIT UNIONS LIQUIDATED IN WISCONSIN FROM 1923 THROUGH JUNE 30, 1940, CLASSIFIED BY AMOUNT OF ASSETS[a]

Amount of Assets	Number of Credit Unions	Percent of Total
none[b]	12	13.6
$1. to $100.99	13	14.8
$101. to $200.99	20	22.7
$201. to $300.99	13	14.8
$301. to $400.99	7	7.9
$401. to $500.99	5	5.7
$501. to $600.99	1	1.1
$601. to $700.99	2	2.3
$701. and over[c]	15	17.1
TOTAL	88[d]	100.0

[a] The amount of assets is taken at the nearest date for which this information could be gotten, prior to dissolution was voted by the membership of the credit union. See text, pp. 148ff.

[b] Includes 9 credit unions which never conducted any business, and 3 credit unions whose charters were revoked.

[c] Includes 2 organizations whose assets were over $701 but under $1,000, 4 whose assets were between $1,450 and $1,900, 1 credit union with assets of $2,829, 4 whose assets ranged between $3,350 and $3,687. The 4 remaining organizations had assets of $8,419, $9,558, $11,120 and $16,703 respectively.

[d] No data available for 3 credit unions that were liquidated.

SOURCE: Files of Wisconsin State Banking Department.

Most of the liquidated credit unions were small. Only 15 percent (13 credit unions) of the number had assets of over $1,000 which is itself a very small amount. Nine credit unions had assets ranging somewhere between $1,000 and $5,000 while 2 had assets in excess of $5,000 but under $10,000, and only 2 were larger than $10,000, the largest having assets of $16,703. About 14 percent (12 credit unions) of the total number had no assets at all, either before or at the time liquidation was voted upon, while about 70 percent of the number liquidated (61 credit unions) had assets varying from $1 to $400. Fifteen percent of the number of unions liquidated were under $101, while 23 percent were between $101 and $200.99

and about 66 percent of the liquidated organizations had assets of $300.99 or under.

The relationship of size of credit union to liquidation was examined by classifying the 18 liquidated unions with assets over $500 at time of liquidation by reason for closing and comparing the results with reason for closing for all liquidated unions. About 25 percent of the large unions' (over $500 in assets) liquidations are accounted for by no interest while a little more than 50 percent of all liquidated unions fell into this category. The larger liquidated unions showed a greater mortality (about 27 percent) due to poor management than did all unions (15 percent). Depression in plant accounted for one-third of the larger unions and only one-fourth for all unions. The frequency of occurrence of embezzlement was somewhat higher in the larger unions than for all unions. There were no cases of company opposition for the larger unions.

One of the factors affecting the size of a credit union is the length of time in existence. Other things being equal, the longer the organization is in existence the more assets it owns. Bearing this relationship in mind, the data just examined seem to point clearly to the conclusion that one reason for the fairly large number of liquidations among Wisconsin credit unions is the lack of discrimination exercised by the Banking Department in extending charters to unions which are, from the very outset, unlikely to succeed because of their limited expansion potentialities. The credit union is positively harmed by this laxity on the part of the chartering body. The true test of the vitality and success of the credit union does not lie in the number of charters granted but in the ability of those organizations which are chartered to perform their functions adequately and for as long as possible.

In order to examine further the relationship between size and liquidations, a frequency distribution of the amount of assets of the total number of credit unions formed from 1923 through December 31, 1939 was computed (Table 42). The frequency distribution of the amount of assets of the 563 credit

TABLE 42

WISCONSIN CREDIT UNIONS LIQUIDATED FROM 1923 TO DECEMBER 31, 1939 CLASSIFIED BY AMOUNT OF ASSETS AND CLASSIFICATION OF CREDIT UNIONS CHARTERED FROM 1923 THROUGH DECEMBER 31, 1939 BY AMOUNT OF ASSETS[a]

	Credit Unions Liquidated		Credit Unions Organized	
Amount of Assets	Number	Percent of Total	Number	Percent of Total
$499.99 and under	67	82.7	125	19.4
$500.00 to $999.99	3	3.7	34	5.3
$1,000.00 to $2,499.99	2	2.5	79	12.3
$2,500.00 to $4,999.99	5	6.2	109	16.9
$5,000.00 to $9,999.99	2	2.5	103	16.0
$10,000.00 to $14,999.99	1	1.2	64	9.9
$15,000.00 to $24,999.99	1	1.2	57	8.9
$25,000.00 and over	..	....	73	11.3
TOTAL	81	100.0	644	100.0

[a] See text p. 150 for procedure.

SOURCE: Files of Wisconsin State Banking Department and 17th *Annual Report on Condition of Credit Unions,* Wisconsin State Banking Commission, (Madison, 1939) p. 13.

unions on December 31, 1939 was taken, to which was added the credit unions liquidated from 1923 through December 31, 1939. While 85 liquidations occurred, 4 were excluded since no data were available, leaving a total of 644 credit unions. Six liquidations which took place after December 31, 1939 are also excluded.

By computing the ratio of the number of credit unions formed of a particular size to the total number of credit unions formed, and comparing this figure with the percent of the total number of liquidated unions of that size, the following results are observed. While only 19 percent of the total number of credit unions formed were under $499.99, about 82 percent of the liquidated unions were of this size. As the unions increased in size, a smaller proportion were liquidated than formed.

About 5 percent of the unions formed had assets of $500.00 to $999.99 which is almost the same proportion as the total number of liquidated unions in this group. Unions having assets in excess of $25,000 comprised about 11 percent of the total number formed but there were no liquidations for organizations of that size or over.

Liquidating Credit Unions by Type of Membership

In order to test the strength of different types of credit union membership, a compilation was made of the number of organizations formed by type of membership from 1923 through 1939. In this connection, it should be pointed out that open-charter credit unions include only those organizations which have a clause in their membership qualifications which states "and such other members as the board of directors may desire." The 85 organizations which were liquidated through December 31, 1939 were classified by type of membership and the ratio of the number liquidating to the number formed in each type of membership was computed.

The worst record is that for open-charter credit unions; nearly two-fifths of such organizations formed were liquidated. While this figure is not startling since other states have experienced the same sort of results, it provides more quantitative information on the weakness resulting from the lack of a common bond or bonds among its membership in this type of organization. Next poorest, judged by the liquidation rate, were associational organizations; approximately one-fourth of the number chartered were liquidated. Breaking down the components of the associational organizations, farm cooperatives showed the highest liquidation rate; 50 percent of the unions formed were liquidated and it is apparent that farm cooperatives are poor fields for organizing credit unions. About 30 percent of the credit unions formed among trade union membership were liquidated while about one-fifth of the parish credit unions formed were subsequently dissolved.

TABLE 43

NUMBER AND PERCENT OF LIQUIDATIONS FROM JANUARY 1, 1923 THROUGH DECEMBER 31, 1939 AMONG WISCONSIN UNIONS CHARTERED THROUGH DECEMBER 31, 1939 CLASSIFIED BY TYPE OF MEMBERSHIP

Type of Membership	Number chartered through Dec. 31, 1939	Number liquidated 1923 through 1939	Percent liquidated to number chartered
Open-charters (community)	18	7	38.8
Associational	127	31	24.4
Occupational	414	43	10.3
Government	72	4	5.5
Educational	16	0	..
TOTAL	647	85	13.1%

SOURCE: Files of Wisconsin State Banking Department.

About 10 percent of the occupational credit unions formed were liquidated while only 5 percent of the organizations formed among government employees were dissolved. Those unions organized among state and federal employees fared best; in neither case did a liquidation occur although 13 of the former and 27 of the latter were chartered, while 11 and 10 percent of municipal and county employees' credit unions were liquidated. One of the best records of survival is displayed by those organizations formed among employees in the field of education; 16 such unions were formed, and none were liquidated.

LIQUIDATING UNIONS CLASSIFIED BY ACTUAL AND POTENTIAL MEMBERSHIP

Further information on the characteristics of liquidated credit unions is presented in Tables 44 and 45 where cross classifications of potential and actual membership as well as actual membership and borrowing members are presented. Table 44 con-

TABLE 44

CREDIT UNIONS LIQUIDATED IN WISCONSIN, CLASSIFIED BY POTENTIAL MEMBERSHIP AND ACTUAL MEMBERSHIP ATTAINED

Potential Membership	Number of liquidated unions	Ratio of Actual to Potential Membership 0-20	20-40	40-60	60-80	80-100
Less than 100	23	5	7	5	4	2
100—199	16	4	7	1	3	1
200—299	8	6	2	..	..	..
300—399	6	3	2	1	..	..
400—499	5	4	1	..	..	..
500—599	3	2	1	..	..	..
600 and over	7	6	1	..	..	..
TOTAL	68	30	21	7	7	3

SOURCE: Files of Wisconsin State Banking Department.

sists of 68 unions [16] of the 91 that were liquidated in Wisconsin through June 30, 1940, while in Table 45, 74 organizations are covered. The figures on potential, actual, and borrowing membership are taken from the latest available report of the credit union before liquidation or wherever possible at the time the membership started to liquidate.

Although some of the reasons for liquidation have little or no relationship to the potential membership, 57 percent of the 68 liquidated unions for which data are available had a potential membership of 199 or less, while 33 percent had a potential membership of 99 or less (Table 44). The number of liquidations declines as the potential membership increases; after 600 or above we find an increase but this can be easily explained. Two liquidations occurred where potential membership is between 800 and 899 while four took place in the potential membership range of 1,000 to 1,499. The reversal of the downward trend in liquidations as potential membership increases is at least partially attributable to the concentration in

16 13 liquidated credit unions which never did any business or whose charters were revoked are excluded, which makes our representation 68 out of a possible 78.

this range of open community credit unions or other types where there is not a close bond,[17] which have a large potential membership since every resident falls into this category, but in fact do not get many actual members.

Since potential membership figures merely show the ceiling on membership, it is necessary to go further in order to see elements of weakness which may cause or contribute to liquidation. In Table 44 the ratio of actual to potential membership by size of potential membership is shown. When potential membership reaches 299 or over there is only one case where actual exceeds 40 percent of potential memberships and in this instance the figure attained is only 47 percent, or in absolute amounts, 176 members.

It is not correct to conclude, however, that the criterion for the potential success of a credit union is the ratio of actual to potential membership attained. As seen in the table, the only cases of a ratio in excess of 60 percent have been obtained where liquidations have been heaviest. It is obviously true that the larger the actual membership the greater the probability of success. Since this is true, if 20 percent of the actual membership of a credit union with 1,000 potential members, joins the organization it would be stronger, other things being equal, to a credit union where 100 percent of the potential entrants join if the potential membership is only 100 members.

From Table 44 it can be seen that there is a reciprocal relationship between the number of members and the number of potential entrants. It would appear that a successful policy for administration of credit unions would call for a very careful and deliberate examination of charter applicants by the credit union supervisory body to determine the actual membership that is likely to be attained by the organization. A widespread policy of careful discrimination in granting charters is called for on the part of the chartering body and this, of course, necessitates a great deal of strength and resistance to criticism

17 Of the seven unions, three are parish, two are open community and two are associational groups.

from well-meaning but misinformed advocates of credit unions who seem to think that all that must be done is grant charters and do so in increasing numbers. The pathological bent for numbers does the credit union movement more harm than good since it plants the seed for subsequent liquidation in very fertile soil.

While figures on potential membership in credit unions and the ratio of actual members to potential entrants shed some light on the inter-relations of membership and liquidations, they do not supply comprehensive information in themselves. Membership figures may be high, but the credit union may not be doing a sufficient volume of business to continue its operations successfully. It is therefore necessary to supplement this data by considering the number of members and the ratio of borrowers to members (Table 45).

TABLE 45

CREDIT UNIONS LIQUIDATED IN WISCONSIN, CLASSIFIED BY ACTUAL MEMBERSHIP AND NUMBER OF BORROWERS

Actual Membership	Number of unions liquidated	Ratio of Borrowers to Actual Membership				
		0-20	20-40	40-60	60-80	80-100
0—25	31	18	1	7	2	3
26—50	24	14	7	2	1	..
51—75	8	2	5	1	..	..
76—100	4	..	2	2	..	..
101—125	1	..	1	..	..	..
126—150	2	1	..	1	..	..
151 and over	4	1	1	2	..	..
TOTAL	74	36	17	15	3	3

SOURCE: Files of Wisconsin State Banking Department.

It is evident from the figures that liquidations decrease as the number of members in the organization increases. The trend is reversed, however, where membership exceeds 150. This is explained by the inclusion of 3 large industrial credit unions and a parish credit union, which were perhaps atypical. Seventy-four percent of the 74 organizations for which data are available had an actual membership of 50 or less. Here is further substantiation of the thesis that credit unions which have a small membership are most vulnerable to liquidation.

By examining the ratio of borrowing members for different sizes of membership some insight is gained into the use of their facilities by members. It is only for those unions with a membership of 25 or less that there are instances of a 100 percent ratio. As the actual membership increases, the ratio of borrowers to members decreases. This would be expected on *a priori* grounds since not all members should be expected to need money at the same time. It is clear from these observations that the actual number of borrowers is important to the success of a credit union and it appears that the authority supervising credit unions must not only examine the possibilities of membership but also the prospective utilization of lending facilities by those members. Such discriminating discernment of course calls for a great deal of insight, skill and care but the credit union's primary function is to take care of the members' needs for funds and if the prospective credit union is not going to be used,—people are not going to borrow—then it would seem wisest not to permit it to receive a charter.

Amounts Paid Out by Liquidating Unions

A liquidation *per se* is not a cause for opprobrium since it may be the result of circumstances outside the control of the organization itself, e. g., the plant closes down or is split up. It would seem that a better indication of the strength of the credit union would be to see whether it is able to return the investments to the shareholders, in addition to meeting all the claims of its creditors.

The final reports submitted by the organizations after liquidation was completed were examined in compiling data on the liquidation record of Wisconsin credit unions. From these reports it was possible to trace the ultimate disbursement of funds and discover how the creditors and owners fared when the organization was dissolved. Data were available for 80 liquidated credit unions while the remaining eleven organizations did not do business at any time, had no loss, and are, therefore, excluded from the discussion since they never existed in an economic sense although they did have a legal existence.

During the liquidation, funds are disbursed first to the creditors of the credit union and the remaining amount is then distributed to the shareholders. If the surplus remaining after creditors are paid off is not sufficient to meet the amount due shareholders, the deficit is pro-rated on the basis of the amount of stock held and the amount is described as "shareholders' assessment." The liquidating dividend is the surplus of assets over liabilities and is not necessarily an indication of the financial strength of the liquidated organization since there are a few instances of unions which did not pay dividends while they were functioning but "plowed" their earnings back into the organization. It would be expected, therefore, that, upon liquidation, they would have a large surplus available for disbursement to their owners.

In every case the creditors received payment in full. In 32 of the 80 organizations examined, the shareholders suffered a loss (were assessed), in 17 cases a dividend was disbursed to shareholders and in 31 cases shareholders received 100 percent payment upon their investments in shares.

While shareholders were assessed in 32 unions, these figures are in themselves meaningless. For the 80 organizations examined the total amount due shareholders was $89,393.20. The amount of actual payment made to these shareholders was $88,364.50; thus 98.8 percent of the amount due was paid, while the difference, only $956.78 was the total monetary loss to shareholders. This figure was 1 percent of the total amount due shareholders and the average assessment per liquidated organization was $29.89. Obviously in those instances where shareholders were assessed, the amounts were small. The largest assessment per union was $214.04 and the next largest was

$144.00. Of the thirty remaining instances where the shareholders were assessed, there is one case amounting to $63.35 while the others range in amounts from $1.75 to $48.60.

In order to measure the incidence of a liquidation upon the members of the organization, the figures for the average loss or gain per member were computed, and are presented in the fifth column of Table 46. The average loss is small, being $2.64

TABLE 46

CREDIT UNIONS LIQUIDATED IN WISCONSIN FROM JANUARY 1923 THROUGH JUNE 30, 1940, CLASSIFIED BY RATIO OF AMOUNT REALIZED TO AMOUNT DUE

Ratio Amount Realized to Amount due	Number of Unions	Percentage of of Total Number of Unions	Total Surplus (+) or Deficit (—)	Average Loss per Member
0 — 19.9% ...	6	7.5	— $209.43	—$2.25
20.0 — 39.9	..	..	..	..
40.0 — 59.9	4	5.0	— 74.11	— 1.24
60.0 — 79.9	7	8.8	— 448.88	— 2.64[a]
80.0 — 99.9	15	18.8	— 224.36	— .59[b]
100.0 — 119.9	43	53.8	+ 1174.72	+ .36[c]
120 and over	5	6.1	+ 1975.36	+ 6.04
			— 956.78	— 1.37
			+ 3150.08	+ 1.01
TOTAL	80	100.0	+$2193.30	+$ .55

[a] Due to inability to obtain figures on membership for one credit union we omitted its loss ($18.20) and used 6 unions.

[b] Due to inability to obtain figures on membership for one credit union we omitted its loss ($18.20) and used 14 unions.

[c] Due to inability to obtain figures on membership for 3 credit unions we omitted them (1 lost $14.97; 1 lost $257.19; the third paid 100 percent of amount due) and used 40 unions.

SOURCE: Files of Wisconsin State Banking Department.

at maximum for unions liquidated with a deficit; the average loss per member for the thirty unions showing a loss is $1.37. The average dividend paid is higher, reaching a high of $6.04 per member and is $1.01 for the 45 unions considered. Subtracting the loss from the surplus and dividing by the total number of liquidated unions, the results of liquidation yielded an average dividend of $.55 per member.

In determining how all 80 unions fared in relation to amounts due and amounts paid, the $3,150.08 realized as dividends by 17 liquidating organizations, was added to the $88,-364.50 realized, and compared with the amount due shareholders. The resulting figure shows that on net balance a gain of $2,193.30 accrued to credit union shareholders who realized 102 percent of the amount due them.

Five percent of the unions liquidated did not pay one cent of the amount due, but the total amount due was small; the sum lost by shareholders in the 4 unions amounted to only $126.58 (Table 46). Two credit unions paid from 10 to 19.9 percent on the amount due creditors and again the losses were small amounting to only $82.85. About 32.6 percent of the liquidated unions paid shareholders amounts varying between 40 and 99.9 percent of the amount due them. Losses here too were small, with $448.88 for the 7 unions paying between 60 and 79.9 percent, being the largest. About 40 percent of the unions paid less than 100 percent of the amounts due their owners.

Sixty percent of the liquidated unions paid their shareholders 100 percent or more of the amount due them. Column 3 of Table 46 shows the surplus in excess of the amounts due and it is noteworthy that these sums exceed the sum of the losses. Over 50 percent of the organizations paid from 100 to 119.9 percent of the amount due while about 6 percent of the liquidated organizations paid 120 percent or more of the amount due shareholders.

In summary, shareholders lost $956.78 but if the surplus of $3,150.08 realized is added, the shareholders *in toto* actually received 2 percent more than the amount due them.

APPENDIX I

Description of a Wisconsin Credit Union

While the organization of credit unions is similar in all states there are certain minor features which are determined by the law under which the union is incorporated. The structure of a Wisconsin credit union is presented in Figure 2.

1. *Members*

Because of the group responsibility for loss it is essential that the members be in close enough contact to enable them to judge accurately the credit standing of those applying for loans. The state Banking Department requires that the organization be formed among persons having a common bond of employment, religious faith, association, etc., and that membership be limited to persons in that group. Applications for membership are presented by one director for vote of the entire board of directors; and after three months and upon the payment of the entrance fee (usually $.25) and the completed purchase of one share of stock the applicant becomes a voting member.

The annual meeting of the credit union must be held in January and each member is entitled only to one vote and no proxy voting is permitted. At this meeting the members elect a board of directors and a credit committee. Special meetings may be called by the board or at the request of 10 percent of the members. Members may decide upon any question of interest to the credit union and, upon appeal of two members, may reverse any decision of the credit committee or board of directors. At a meeting specifically announced for the purpose the members may, by a vote of three-fourths of those present, amend the by-laws or remove any officer, member of the credit committee or board of directors and fill the vacancy caused by the removal.

2. *Board of Directors*

At the first meeting and thereafter at each annual meeting, the members shall elect a board of at least five members. Any member with one fully paid share is eligible for election and serves without compensation. The terms are staggered so that at least one new officer is elected every year. Meetings of the board must be held once a month, or more often if called by the president or any three members. The functions of the board are as follows:

a. Elect from their number a president, a vice-president, a secretary and a treasurer who are executive officers.
b. Act as general managers of the affairs, funds and records of the corporation.
c. Act upon all applications for membership.
d. Act upon the expulsion of members.
e. Fix the amount of surety bond which is required of each officer having custody of funds.
f. Make recommendations to meetings of the members pertaining to matters which in their opinion members should decide.
g. Approve loan applications made by members of the credit committee.
h. At the close of the fiscal year the board or a committee chosen from its members shall make a thorough audit of the corporation's books and report its findings at the annual meeting.
i. Declare dividends.
j. Borrow money as outlined by Statute.
k. Present dissolution proposal to members if unanimously approved by the board.

3. *Credit Committee*

The credit committee of at least three men is chosen by the members for staggered terms of three years and may receive compensation for their services. This committee approves every loan or advance made by the union except where a committee man is the applicant, and the loan must be considered provident before it is approved. The committee shall also decide upon the adequacy of collateral to secure a loan and may grant extensions on loans but in no case can any member endorse a note for a borrower.

4. *President*

The president presides at meetings of the members and of the board of directors and performs other customary duties connected with the office as well as those assigned by the board.

5. *Vice-President*

This officer shall in the absence of the president perform the duties of the president and such other duties as the board may prescribe.

6. *Treasurer*

The Treasurer is custodian of the funds, securities, books of account and all valuable papers of the credit union and shall keep the books in accord with and open to the inspection of the state Banking Commission. He shall furnish a bond in any amount set by the directors which shall be paid for by the credit union. At the end of each month, he shall prepare a balance sheet of the credit union, which shall be countersigned by the president and posted for the benefit of the members. He shall deposit all funds in banks of deposit prescribed by the board of directors and keep a receipt of all payments or withdrawals of money.

7. *Secretary*

This officer keeps records of all meetings of the members and board and shall give notice of all meetings and perform all other duties demanded by his office.

Within the limits specified in the law, the board may compensate these officers for their services rendered. In addition, the credit union may employ additional paid help if the volume of business warrants such help. This help is appointed by the board.

8. *Clerks*

One or more clerks may be hired to assist the secretary, to keep the credit union's books and any other duties assigned by the board; they need not be members of the credit union.

9. *Assistant Treasurer*

This employee serves as assistant to the Treasurer, or takes over his duties in his absence. He must be bonded, need not be a member of the union and his compensation as an employee is fixed by the board.

10. *Other Employees*

The board may if it is in the interest of the credit union hire any additional help needed to operate the organization.

11. *Publicity Director*

In order to increase the membership of their credit union, the board of directors of some organizations have chosen a publicity director from the membership. He is called upon to devote a portion of his free time to soliciting new membership among the group which is eligible to join, and publicizing the credit union's loan facilities among the members to stimulate borrowing by the members.

12. *Membership Committee*

In some credit unions a membership committee, usually of five members (two directors and three of the more active and interested members) is appointed by the board of directors to serve with or in place of a publicity director with similar functions. Monthly reports to the board are required from the chairman of this committee and since service is time-consuming it is considered advisable to select a new group every two or three months.

FIGURE 2

ORGANIZATION OF WISCONSIN CREDIT UNION

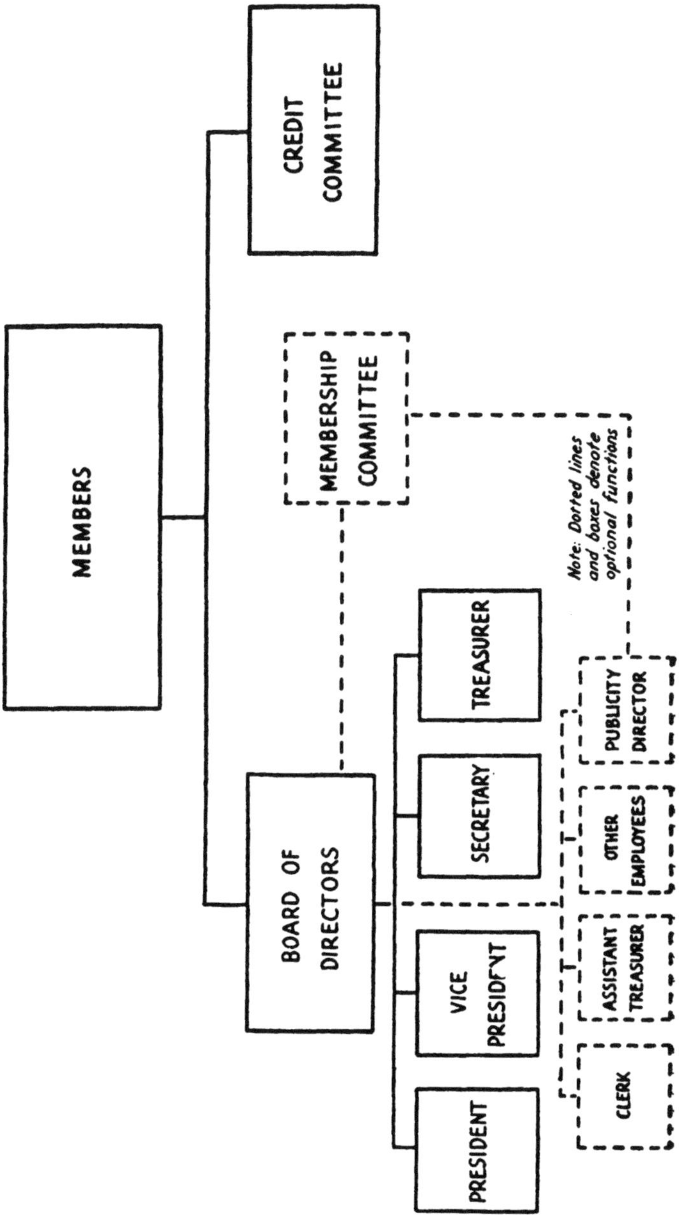

APPENDIX II

TABLE 47

WISCONSIN CREDIT UNIONS CLASSIFIED BY AGE AND SIZE
DECEMBER 31, 1939
AGE (IN FULL CALENDAR YEARS)[a]

Total Assets (in dollars)	Less than 1	1	2	3	4	5	6	7	8	9	10	Over 10	Total
Less than 500	28	7	6	5	7	2	1	2					58
500 — 999.99	9	6	2	6	2	2		2	1	1			31
1,000 — 2,499.99	3	18	9	14	15	7	2	7	2				77
2,500 — 4,999.99	3	16	16	17	16	14	6	12	3	1			104
5,000 — 9,999.99		7	7	18	22	12	16	12	7				101
10,000 — 14,999.99		5	2	3	12	10	12	10	4	4		1	63
15,000 — 24,999.99		1	3	6	10	9	12	9	2	1	1	2	56
25,000 — 99,999.99		1	1	4	7	11	17	8	5			3	57
100,000 — 249,999.99				1	1	2	6	1				1	12
250,000 — 499,999.99						1	1					1	3
500,000 and over												1	1
TOTAL	43	61	46	74	92	70	73	63	24	7	1	9	563

[a] The figure 1 means 1 but less than 2 years of operation as of December 31, 1939. The credit unions are classified by age as of the date on which the articles of incorporation were approved by the Banking Commission. In a few instances the age is overstated. This occurs where a union's articles of incorporation are dated at the end of the year but it does not commence operations until the early part of the following year although the age is recorded in the above table from the date articles were approved.

SOURCE: Files of Wisconsin State Banking Department.

INDEX

Bei Fragen zur Produktsicherheit wenden Sie sich bitte an:
If you have any questions regarding product safety,
please contact:

Walter de Gruyter GmbH
Genthiner Straße 13
10785 Berlin
productsafety@degruyterbrill.com